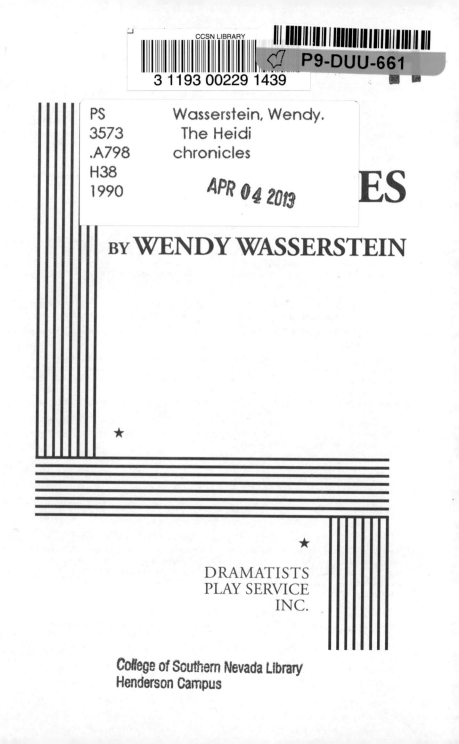

ES

BY WENDY WASSERSTEIN

DRAMATISTS
PLAY SERVICE
INC.

THE HEIDI CHRONICLES
Copyright © 1990, Wendy Wasserstein

SPECIAL NOTE

SPECIAL NOTE ON SONGS AND RECORDINGS

SPECIAL NOTE ON SLIDES

Color slides of the paintings mentioned in this Play, along with a cue sheet, can be obtained from Mom's Idea Hut, 235 Bull Road, Washingtonville, NY 10992. Telephone: 845-496-7949. Fax: 845-496-0902. Email: ideahut@aol.com. Please contact them directly for rental fees.

For Christopher

THE HEIDI CHRONICLES was first presented in New York City by Playwrights Horizons (Andre Bishop, Artistic Director; Paul S. Daniels, Executive Director) on December 12, 1988. It was directed by Daniel Sullivan; the set design was by Thomas Lynch; costume design was by Jennifer Von Mayrhauser; lighting design was by Pat Collins; and the sound design was by Scott Lehrer. The production stage manager was Roy Harris; and the production manager was Carl Mulert. The cast, in order of appearance, was as follows:

HEIDI HOLLAND . . . . Joan Allen
SUSAN JOHNSTON . . . . Ellen Parker
PETER PATRONE . . . . Boyd Gaines
SCOOP ROSENBAUM . . . . Peter Friedman
CHRIS BOXER, MARK, EASTER BUNNY,
WAITER, RAY . . . . Drew McVety
JILL, DEBBIE, LISA, HOSTESS . . . . Anne Lange
FRAN, MOLLY, BETSY, APRIL . . . . Joanne Camp
BECKY, CLARA, DENISE . . . . Sarah Jessica Parker

The production subsequently transferred to the Plymouth Theatre, on Broadway, on March 9, 1989. The only cast change was Cynthia Nixon, who took over the roles of BECKY, CLARA, and DENISE.

THE HEIDI CHRONICLES was first performed in a workshop at the Seattle Repertory Theatre, Seattle, Washington, in April, 1988. The director was Daniel Sullivan. The cast was as follows:

HEIDI HOLLAND . . . . Lizbeth Mackay
SUSAN JOHNSTON . . . . Caroline Aaron
CHRIS, MARK, WAITER, RAY . . . . Peter Lohnes
PETER PATRONE . . . . Jack Gilpin
SCOOP ROSENBAUM . . . . Alan Rosenberg
FRAN, LISA, APRIL . . . . Gretchen Corbett
JILL, DEBBIE, MOLLY, PAULA . . . . . . Susy Schneider
BECKY, CLARA, DENISE . . . . Martha Plimpton

ACT ONE

Prologue: A lecture hall, New York, 1989
Scene 1: Chicago, 1965
Scene 2: Manchester, New Hampshire, 1968
Scene 3: Ann Arbor, Michigan, 1970
Scene 4: Chicago, 1974
Scene 5: New York, 1977

ACT TWO

All scenes take place in New York.
Prologue: A lecture hall, 1989
Scene 1: An apartment, 1980
Scene 2: A TV studio, 1982
Scene 3: A restaurant, 1984
Scene 4: The Plaza Hotel, 1986
Scene 5: A pediatrics ward, 1987
Scene 6: An apartment, 1989

The production by Playwrights Horizons, Inc. was awarded a major grant from The Fund for New American Plays, a project of The John F. Kennedy Center for the Performing Arts with support from the American Express Company in cooperation with the President's Committee on the Arts and the Humanities.

AUTHOR'S NOTE

Because of the episodic nature of The Heidi Chronicles, the most successful production in my mind is one in which the transitions appear seamless. In the Playwrights Horizons production the quick changes were solved by the use of a periaktoi. Under Daniel Sullivan's direction music from a previous scene was used as transition into the next. Moreover, in more elaborate productions slides can be used between scenes. Again, in Daniel Sullivan's Broadway production slides of women's images in painting and college life were shown between Act One Scene Two and Three. Those of women's and gay marches of the period were used between Act One Scene Four and Five, and imaginary BOOMER Magazine covers were shown between Act Two Scene Two and Three. However, I wish to remind future productions that The Heidi Chronicles began in a workshop situation at The Seattle Repertory Theatre. The key to the play is not in mounting nostalgic accoutrements, but in moving the chronicle forward as swiftly and simply as possible.

W.W.

THE HEIDI CHRONICLES

PROLOGUE

1989, lecture hall, Columbia University. Heidi, behind podium, right of screen. During the lecture slides of the paintings appear on the screen.

HEIDI. Sofonisba Anguissola painted this portrait of her sister, Minerva, in 1559. Not only was Sofonisba a painter with an international reputation, but so were her six sisters. Here's half the family in Sofonisba's "Three Sisters Playing Chess" painted in 1555. (*Heidi looks up at the painting.*) "Hello, Girls." Although Sofonisba was praised in the seventeenth century as being a portraitist equal to Titian, and at least thirty of her paintings remain known to us, there is no trace of her or any other woman artist prior to the twentieth century in your current Art History Survey textbook. Of course, in my day, this same standard text mentioned no women, "from the Dawn of History to the Present." Are you with me? Okay.

Clara Peeters, roughly 1594–1657, whose undated self portrait we see here, was I believe the greatest woman artist of the seventeenth century. And now I'd like you to name ten others. Peeters work predates the great period of Northern still life painting. In her breakfast paintings, Clara's term not mine, she used more geometry and less detail than her male peers. Notice here the cylindrical silver canister, the disc of the plate, and the triangular cuts in the cheese. Trust me. This is cheese. After breakfast, in fact, Clara went through a prolonged cheese period.

A leap, but go with me. "We Both Must Fade," painted in 1869 by the American genre painter Lily Martin Spencer combines in a "vanitas" painting the formal portraiture of

Sofonisba and the still life composition of Peeters. We have a young woman posing in an exquisitely detailed dress surrounded by symbolic still life objects. The fading flower and the timepiece are both reminders of mortality and time passing. While the precious jewelry spilling out is an allusion to the transcience of earthly possessions. This portrait can be perceived as a meditation on the brevity of youth, beauty and life. But what can't?

Okay to the vital issue at hand. How to remember these paintings for next week's midterm. Sofonisba Anguissola, formal portraiture in the style of Titian with a taste for red jewelry, Clara Peeters, Flemish still life master of geometry and cheese, and as for Mrs. Lily Martin Spencer and "We Both Must Fade." Frankly, this painting has always reminded me of me at one of those horrible high school dances. And you sort of want to dance, and you sort of want to go home, and you sort of don't know what you want. So you hang around, a fading rose in an exquisitely detailed dress, waiting to see what might happen.

END OF PROLOGUE

SCENE 1

1965, a high school dance. Folding chairs, streamers, and a table with a punch bowl. Two sixteen-year-old girls enter. Susan, wearing a skirt and button-down sweater, and Heidi in a traditional dress. The girls look out at the dance floor as they sing and sway to the music. "The Shoop Shoop Song" is playing.*

SUSAN. (*Singing.*) "Is it in his eyes?"
HEIDI. (*Singing.*) "Oh nooooooo, you'll be deceived."
SUSAN. (*Singing.*) "Is it in his eyes?"
HEIDI. (*Singing.*) "Oh, no, he'll make believe."*
SUSAN. Heidi! Heidi! Look at the guy over at the radiator.
HEIDI. Which one?

---

*Used by permission. See note on page 81.

SUSAN. In the blue jeans, tweed jacket and the weejuns.

HEIDI. They're all wearing that.

SUSAN. The one in the vest, blue jeans, the tweed jacket and the weejuns.

HEIDI. Cute.

SUSAN. Looks kinda like Bobby Kennedy.

HEIDI. Kinda. Yup, he's definitely cute.

SUSAN. Look! He can twist and smoke at the same time. I love that! (*Susan unbuttons her sweater and pulls a necklace out of her purse.*)

HEIDI. Susie, what are you doing?

SUSAN. Heidi, men rely on first impressions. Oh, God, he's incredible! Heidi, move!

HEIDI. What, Susie?

SUSAN. Just move!! The worst thing you can do is cluster. 'Cause then it looks like you just wanna hang around with your girlfriend. But don't look desperate. Men don't dance with desperate women. Oh my God! There's one coming. Will you start moving!! Trust me. (*Heidi begins to move. She doesn't notice a boy, Chris Boxer, who comes over to her.*)

CHRIS. Hi.

HEIDI. Hi.

CHRIS. Hi, I'm Chris Boxer, Student Council president here.

HEIDI. I'm Heidi Holland. Editor of the newspaper somewhere else.

CHRIS. Great. I knew I could talk to you. Do you want to dance?

HEIDI. I'm sorry. I can't leave my girlfriend. (*She moves back to Susan.*)

SUSAN. I don't believe this.

HEIDI. This is my girlfriend, Susan Johnston. We came to the dance together.

CHRIS. Oh, I thought you were alone.

SUSAN. Actually, we just met.

CHRIS. Well, very nice to meet you both. (*He begins to walk away.*)

SUSAN. Chris, don't go.

HEIDI. Please don't go. We can all dance together. We can form a line and hully gully, baby.

CHRIS. Well, that's the headmaster. I guess I have to go and uh, ask him how it's going. Keep the faith. (*He snaps his fingers.*)

HEIDI. We will. (*He begins to walk away. Susan calls after him.*)

SUSAN. Nice meeting you. (*Susan begins whispering to Heidi.*) I can't believe you did that. Heidi, we're at a dance! You know, girl meets boy. They hold hands walking in the sand. Then they go to the Chapel of Love. Get it?

HEIDI. Got it.

VOICEOVER. The next dance is going be a Ladies' Choice.

SUSAN. All right! Let's get organized here. Heidi, stand in front of me. I can't ask "twist and smoke" to dance with my skirt this long. What should I say to him? (*Susan rolls up skirt.*)

HEIDI. Ask him how he coordinates the twisting with the smoking.

SUSAN. You know, as your best friend, I must tell you frankly that you're going to get really messed up unless you learn to take men seriously.

HEIDI. Susan, there is absolutely no difference between you and me and him. Except that he can twist and smoke at the same time and we can get out of gym with an excuse called "I have my monthly."

SUSAN. Shit! It's still too long. (*She continues to roll up the waist of her skirt.*) Can you get home all right by yourself?

HEIDI. He'll never even suspect I know you.

SUSAN. Wish me luck!

HEIDI. (*Kisses her on the cheek.*) Luck!

SUSAN. (*Jumps back in horror.*) Heidi!!!! Don't!

HEIDI. Keep the faith! (*She snaps her fingers as Chris Boxer did.*)

SUSAN. Shhhhh! Don't make me laugh or my skirt will roll down.

HEIDI. I'll call you tomorrow. (*Susan exits as she waves good-bye to Heidi. Heidi sits on a chair, takes out a book and puts it on her lap as she stares out as "Play with Fire" begins to play.* Peter, a young man in a St. Mark's School blazer, approaches. He looks at her. She smiles and looks down.*)

PETER. You must be very bright.

---

*Used by permission.

10

HEIDI. Excuse me?

PETER. You look so bored you must be very bright.

HEIDI. I'm sorry?

PETER. Don't be sorry. I appreciate bored people. Bored, depressed, anxious. These are the qualities I look for in a woman. Your ladyfriend is dancing with the gentleman who looks like Bobby Kennedy. I find men who smoke and twist at the same time so dreary.

HEIDI. Not worth the coordination, really.

PETER. Do you have any?

HEIDI. I can sit and read at the same time.

PETER. What book is that?

HEIDI. *Death, Be Not Proud.*

PETER. Of course.

HEIDI. A favorite of mine at dances.

PETER. I was drawn to you from the moment I saw you shielding that unfortunate wench rolling up her garments in the tempest.

HEIDI. I'm sorry.

PETER. Please. Don't apologize for being the most attractive woman on this cruise.

HEIDI. Cruise?

PETER. She docks tonight in Portsmouth. And then farewell to The Queen Mary. Forever to harbor in Long Beach, California. C'est triste, n'est pas?

HEIDI. Ce n'est pas bon.

PETER. (*Excited.*) Our tragic paths were meant to cross. I leave tomorrow for the sanitorium in Zurich. (*He coughs.*)

HEIDI. How odd. I'm going to the sanitorium in Milan. (*She coughs.*)

PETER. My parents are heartbroken. They thought I was entering Williams College in the fall.

HEIDI. My parents put down a deposit at Vassar.

PETER. We've only this night together. I'm Peter, a small noise from Winnetka. I tried to pick out your name . . . Amanda, Lady Clara, Estelle.

HEIDI. It's . . .

PETER. No, don't tell me. I want to remember you as you are. Here beside me in the moonlight, the stars above us . . .

11

HEIDI. The sea below us.

PETER. Glenn Miller and the orchestra. It's all so peaceful.

HEIDI. Mmmmmm. Quite peaceful. (*The "Shoop Shoop Song" begins playing.*)

PETER. The twist and smokers are heaving themselves on their ladyfriends. This must be the final song. Would you do me the honor of one dance? (*He takes her hand to rise.*)

HEIDI. Certainly.

PETER. Ahhh! "The Shoop Shoop Song." Baroque but fragile.

HEIDI. Melodic but atonal.

PETER. Will you marry me?

HEIDI. I covet my independence.

PETER. Perhaps when you leave the sanatorium, you'll think otherwise. I want to know you all my life. If we can't marry, let's be great friends.

HEIDI. I will keep your punch cup as a memento beside my pillow.

PETER. Well, shall we hully gully, baby?

HEIDI. Really, I . . .

PETER. Don't worry. I'll teach you. (*He begins to do some form of line dance. He holds Heidi's hand and instructs her. They sing as they dance together.*) "How 'bout the way he acts?" (*He points to Heidi.*)

HEIDI. "Oh noooo, that's not the way." (*She begins to giggle.*)

PETER. "And you're not listenin' to what I say. If you wanna know if he loves you so . . ." (*He takes Heidi's waist and twirls her.*) "It's in his kiss."

HEIDI AND PETER. "Oh yeah!!!! It's in his kiss!!" (*They continue to dance offstage as the lights fade.*)*

END SCENE

SCENE 2

1968, a dance. There are "Eugene McCarthy for President" signs. A Janis Joplin and Big Brother and the Holding Company song like "Take A Piece of My Heart"

*Used by permission. See note on page 81.

is playing.* A hippie in a Sgt. Pepper jacket smokes a joint and when Heidi enters he offers her a drag. Heidi, wearing a floral shawl, refuses and stands by the food table. Scoop Rosenbaum, slightly intense but charismatic in blue jeans and workshirt, comes over to her. He takes a beer from a bucket on stage.

SCOOP. Are you guarding the chips?
HEIDI. No.
SCOOP. Then you're being very difficult.
HEIDI. Please, help yourself.
SCOOP. Where are you going?
HEIDI. I'm trying to listen to the music.
SCOOP. Janis Joplin and Big Brother and the Holding Company. "A—" singer. "C+" band. Far less innovative than the Kinks. You know, you really have one hell of an inferiority complex.
HEIDI. I do?
SCOOP. Sure. I have no right to say you're difficult. Don't you believe in human dignity? I mean, you're obviously a liberal or you wouldn't be here.
HEIDI. I came with a friend.
SCOOP. You came to Manchester, New Hampshire in a blizzard to ring doorbells for Gene McCarthy because of a friend? Why the fuck didn't you go skiing instead?
HEIDI. I don't ski. (*Scoop offers Heidi a potato chip.*)
SCOOP. "B—" texture. "C+" crunch. You go to one of those Seven Sister schools?
HEIDI. How did you know?
SCOOP. You're all concerned citizens.
HEIDI. I told you, I came because of a friend.
SCOOP. That's bullshit. Be real. You're neat and clean for Eugene. You think if you go door to door and ring bells, this sucker will become president and we'll all be good people and wars in places you've never heard of before will end, and everyone will have enough to eat and send their daughters to Vassar. Like I said, neat and clean for Eugene.
HEIDI. Would you excuse me? (*Scoop smiles and extends his hand to her.*)

---

*See Special Note on copyright page.

13

SCOOP. It's been lovely chatting with me.

HEIDI. A pleasure.

SCOOP. What's your name?

HEIDI. Susan.

SCOOP. Susan what?

HEIDI. Susan Johnston. See ya.

SCOOP. Hey, Susan Johnston, wouldn't you like to know who I am?

HEIDI. Uh . . .

SCOOP. C'mon, nice girl like you isn't going to look a man in the eye and tell him, "I have absolutely no interest in you. You've been incredibly obnoxious and your looks are 'B—'."

HEIDI. Why do you grade everything?

SCOOP. I used to be a very good student.

HEIDI. Used to?

SCOOP. I dropped out of Princeton. The Woodrow Wilson School of International Bullshit.

HEIDI. That's admirable. So what do you do now?

SCOOP. This and that. Here and there.

HEIDI. You work for McCarthy? Well, you are at a McCarthy dance.

SCOOP. I came with a friend. Susan, don't you know this is just the tip of the iceberg? McCarthy is irrelevant. He's a "C+" Adlai Stevenson. The changes in this country could be enormous. Beyond anything your sister mind can imagine.

HEIDI. Are you a real-life radical?

SCOOP. You mean, do I make bombs in my parents' West Hartford basement? Susan, how could I be a radical? I played lacrosse at Exeter and I'm a Jew whose first name is Scoop. You're not very good at nuance. And you're too eager to categorize. I'm a journalist. I'm just here to have a look around.

HEIDI. Do you work for a paper?

SCOOP. Did they teach you at Vassar to ask so many inane questions in order to keep a conversation going?

HEIDI. Well, like I said. I have to meet my friend.

SCOOP. Me, too. I have to meet Paul Newman.

HEIDI. Please tell him Susan says "hi."

SCOOP. You don't believe I have to meet Paul Newman.

HEIDI. I'm sure you do.

14

SCOOP. I'm picking him up at the airport and taking him and Mr. McCarthy to a press conference. Paul's a great guy. Why don't you come drinking with us? We can rap over a few brews.

HEIDI. I'm sorry. I can't.

SCOOP. Why not?

HEIDI. I just can't.

SCOOP. Susan, let me get this straight. You would rather drive back to Poughkeepsie with five virgins in a Volkswagon discussing Norman Mailer and birth control on dangerous frozen roads than go drinking with Eugene McCarthy, Paul Newman and Scoop Rosenbaum? You're cute, Susan. Very cute.

HEIDI. And you are really irritating!!

SCOOP. That's the first honest thing you've said all night! Lady, you better learn to stand up for yourself. I'll let you in on a scoop from Scoop.

HEIDI. Did they teach you construction like that at Princeton?

SCOOP. I dig you, Susan. I dig you a lot.

HEIDI. Can we say "like" instead of "dig"? I mean, while I'm standing up for myself . . .

SCOOP. I like you, Susan. You're prissy, but I like you a lot.

HEIDI. Well, I don't know if I like you.

SCOOP. Why should you like me? I'm arrogant and difficult. But I'm very smart. So you'll put up with me. What?

HEIDI. What what?

SCOOP. You're thinking something.

HEIDI. Actually, I was wondering what mothers teach their sons that they never bother to tell their daughters.

SCOOP. What do you mean?

HEIDI. I mean, why the fuck are you so confident?

SCOOP. Ten points for Susan.

HEIDI. Have we moved on to points from letter grades?

SCOOP. There's hope for you. You're going to be quite the little politico.

HEIDI. I'm planning to be an art historian.

SCOOP. Please don't say that. That's really suburban.

HEIDI. I'm interested in the individual expression of the human soul. Content over form.

SCOOP. But I thought the point of contemporary art is that the form becomes the content. Look at Albers' "Homage to A Square." Three superimposed squares and we're talking perception, integration, isolation. Just three squares and they reflect the gross inadequacies of our society. Therefore, your argument is inconclusive.

HEIDI. Don't give me a Marxist interpretation of Albers.

SCOOP. You really are one fuck of a liberal! Next thing you'll tell me is how much Herbert Marcuse means to you. What?

HEIDI. Nothing.

SCOOP. I don't fuckin' believe it! You've never read Marcuse!

HEIDI. Isn't Paul Newman waiting for you, Scoop?

SCOOP. Isn't your friend waiting for you, *Heidi*? (*Scoop jumps up.*) Basket, Rosenbaum. 30 points. The score is 30 to 10.

HEIDI. How did you know my name?

SCOOP. I told you I'm a journalist. Do you really think anything gets by *The Liberated Earth News*?

HEIDI. That's your paper!!

SCOOP. Editor-in-chief. Circulation 362 and growing. Okay. Truth. I know your name is Heidi because it says so (*He points to her breast.*) right there on your name tag. Heidi. "H-E-I-D-I."

HEIDI. (*Embarrassed.*) Oh!

SCOOP. Oh!!!!

HEIDI. Oh well . . . (*She begins to pull the tag off.*)

SCOOP. You don't have to look at the floor.

HEIDI. I'm not.

SCOOP. I've got nothing on you so far. Why are you so afraid to speak up?

HEIDI. I'm not afraid to speak up.

SCOOP. Heidi, you don't understand. You're the one this is all going to affect. You're the one whose life this will all change significantly. Has to. You're a very serious person. In fact, you're the unfortunate contradiction in terms—a serious good person. And I envy you that.

HEIDI. Thank you. I guess.

SCOOP. Yup. You'll be one of those true believers who

16

didn't understand it was just a phase. The Trotskyite during Lenin's New Economic policy. The worshipper of fallen images in Christian Judea.

HEIDI. And you?

SCOOP. Me? I told you. I'm just here to have a look around.

HEIDI. What if you get left behind?

SCOOP. You mean if after all the politics you girls decide to go "hog wild," demanding equal pay, equal rights, equal orgasms?

HEIDI. All people deserve to fulfill their potential.

SCOOP. Absolutely.

HEIDI. I mean, why should some well-educated woman waste her life making you and your children tuna fish sandwiches?

SCOOP. She shouldn't. And for that matter, neither should a badly educated woman. Heidella, I'm on your side.

HEIDI. Don't call me "Heidella." It's diminutive.

SCOOP. You mean "demeaning," and it's not. It's endearing.

HEIDI. You're deliberately eluding my train of thought.

SCOOP. No, I'm subtly asking you to go to bed with me . . . before I go meet Paul Newman. (*Covered pause.*)

HEIDI. Oh.

SCOOP. You have every right to say no. I can't guarantee absolute equality of experience.

HEIDI. I can take care of myself, thanks.

SCOOP. You've already got the lingo down, kiddo. Pretty soon you'll be burning bras.

HEIDI. Maybe I'll go "hog wild."

SCOOP. I hope so. Are you a virgin?

HEIDI. Excuse me?

SCOOP. If you choose to accept this mission, I'll find out one way or the other.

HEIDI. (*Embarrassed.*) That's okay.

SCOOP. Why do you cover your mouth when you talk about sex?

HEIDI. Hygiene. (*She laughs nervously. Scoop takes her hand away from her mouth.*)

SCOOP. I told you. You're a serious good person. And I'm honored. Maybe you'll think fondly of all this in some Prous-

17

tian haze when you're thirty-five and picking your daughter up from The Ethical Culture School to escort her to cello class before dinner with Dad, the noted psychiatrist and Miro poster collector.

HEIDI. No. I'll be busy torching lingerie.

SCOOP. Maybe I'll remember it one day when I'm thirty-five and watching my son's performance as Johnny Appleseed. Maybe I'll look at my wife who puts up with me and flash on when I was editor of a crackpot liberal newspaper and thought I could fall in love with Heidi Holland, the canvassing art historian, that first snowy night in Manchester, New Hampshire, 1968.

HEIDI. Are you guarding the chips?

SCOOP. No. I trust them. (*He kisses her passionately as a song like "White Rabbit" begins playing.* Scoop then looks at his watch and gathers his coat. He begins to leave the room and turns back to Heidi. She looks at her watch and follows him.*)

END SCENE

SCENE 3

1970, a church basement in Ann Arbor, Michigan. Jill, 40, immaculate in a whale turtleneck and pleated skirt, and Fran, 30, in army fatigues, are setting out Danish and coffee while Aretha Franklin's "Respect" blares in the background.** Fran dances and sings along, "Sock it to me. sock it to me."

JILL. (*Tasting a cookie.*) Fran, I think it would be much cozier if we met next time in one of our homes.

FRAN. Jill, we're not the fuckin' Junior League.

JILL. I just hope that everyone is comfortable here. (*She begins moving the chairs.*) Maybe we should rearrange things and make a conversation nook.

FRAN. You sound like my fuckin' mother. She decorates with sheets. (*Fran begins to arrange chairs. Becky, 17, in blue*

---

*See Special Note on copyright page.

* *Used by permission. See note on page 81.

18

jeans and a poncho, has entered while they are moving and singing. Fran looks up, notices her.) Hi there.

JILL. Hi.

FRAN. We're just getting into the mood. (*She shuts off the music.*) All right, A-RE-THA!

JILL. Can we help you?

BECKY. Sure. I'm Becky Groves. I saw your poster upstairs. (*Jill and Fran immediately go over to Becky and embrace her.*)

JILL. Becky, I'm Jill and I'm *so* glad you came.

FRAN. Becky, I'm Fran and I'm *so* glad you came. (*Jill brings a plate of cookies over to Becky.*)

JILL. Becky, how 'bout a peanut butter granola cookie? We each take turns providing the goodies.

FRAN. "Goodies"? Jill, we're also not the fuckin' Brownies.

BECKY. I sometimes call sweets and cookies "goodies."

JILL. Thank you, Becky.

FRAN. Becky, please tell me if I come on a little strong. I'm trying to work through that.

JILL. I love you, Fran. (*Heidi and Susan enter. Both wear blue jeans, hiking boots, and down jackets.*)

SUSAN. Sorry. Sorry. I'm sorry we're late. Those snow drifts are mammoth.

FRAN. Bigger than Aphrodite's tits. (*Fran and Jill go to embrace Susan and Heidi.*)

JILL. Hello, Susan. It's *so* good to see you.

FRAN. Hello, Susan. It's *so* good to see you.

SUSAN. This is my friend Heidi. She's visiting for the week.

JILL. Hello, Heidi. It's *so* good to see you.

FRAN. This is Becky, who is joining us this week.

SUSAN. (*Embracing Becky.*) Hello, Becky. It's *so* good to see you.

FRAN. All right! Let the good times roll! (*They all sit down. Heidi moves her chair and sits slightly outside of the circle behind Fran.*)

JILL. I'd like to call to order this meeting of the Huron Street Ann Arbor Consciousness Raising Rap Group. Heidi, Becky, since you're new I want you to know that everything here is very free, very easy. I've been a member of the group for about five months, now. I'm a mother of four daughters and when I first came I was, as Fran would say, "a fuckin'

19

Hostess cupcake." Everybody in my life — my husband Bill, my daughters, my friends — could lean on perfect Jill. The only problem was there was one person I had completely forgotten to take care of.

BECKY. Who was that?

JILL. Jill.

BECKY. I feel that way sometimes.

SUSAN. We all feel that way sometimes.

BECKY. You do?

FRAN. No, we grow up on fuckin' "Father Knows Best" and we think we have rights! You think Jane Wyatt demanded clitoral stimulation from Robert Young? No fuckin' way. *(Heidi moves her chair further away from the circle.)*

SUSAN. I love you, Fran.

JILL. I love you, too, Fran.

FRAN. *(Primping.)* Maybe I should dress for combat more often.

SUSAN. Fran, sometimes I think you let your defensiveness overwhelm your tremendous vulnerability.

JILL. Heidi, Becky, you should know that Fran is a gifted physicist, and a lesbian, and we support her choice to sleep with women.

BECKY. Sure.

FRAN. Do you support my choice, Heidi?

HEIDI. I'm just visiting.

FRAN. I have to say right now that I don't feel comfortable with a "just visiting" in the room. I need to be able to come here and reach out to you as my sisters. Okay, Heidi-ho?

HEIDI. Okay.

FRAN. Just don't judge us. Christ, we spend our lives having men judge us. All right, let the good times roll!

SUSAN. I'll start. This week I think I made a little headway, but I'm also afraid I fell back a few paces.

JILL. Susie, what did you decide to do about *The Law Review*?

SUSAN. I accepted the position!

JILL. Good.

SUSAN. Becky, I was seriously considering beginning a law journal devoted solely to women's legal issues. But after some pretty heavy deliberation, I've decided to work within the male establishment power base to change the system.

20

JILL. Susan, I'm so proud of you for making a choice.

SUSAN. Do you know my mother would have married me because I have this position?

FRAN. What are you bullshitting about? "You're going to work from within the male establishment power base." And I'm going to date fuckin' Tricia Nixon. Susan, either you shave your legs or you don't.

SUSAN. I love you, Fran.

FRAN. I scare the shit out of you, Susan.

BECKY. Why are you yelling at her?

SUSAN. Becky, Fran is one of the most honest people I've ever met. She's a great friend.

BECKY. Well, she sounds kinda like Bobby.

JILL. Who's Bobby?

BECKY. Well, Bobby's my boyfriend. Well, we kinda live together. Well, my father and mother split up last year. My father is in the film department here and last year he made this documentary called "Flower Children of Ypsilanti." It won a whole bunch of awards and stuff.

HEIDI. Is your father Ed Groves? That's a great documentary.

BECKY. You saw it?

HEIDI. I'm a graduate student. That means I go to a lot of movies.

BECKY. Well, remember that blonde girl with all the rope bracelets who wanted to go to San Francisco so she could sleep with Donovan? Well, she's my father's other wife.

FRAN. Fuckin' mellow yellow.

SUSAN. That's illegal.

BECKY. They're not really married. She just kinda wears his ring. Anyway, when he left, my mom flipped out. So she went to Esalen in California. I think she's talking to a tree or something. She was only going for a week, but it's been six months. So I asked Bobby to move in, at least until I finished high school, but it's kinda not working. But I don't know.

JILL. You don't know what?

BECKY. I mean, I try to be super nice to him. I make all his meals, and I never disagree with him. But then he just gets angry or stoned. So when I need to think things through, I lock the bathroom door and cry. But I try not to make any

21

sounds. (*Pause.*) Now you're all going to hate me, right?

FRAN. Lamb, no one here is ever going to hate you.

JILL. Becky, would you like to stay with me and my family for a while?

FRAN. I love you, Jill.

SUSAN. I love you, Jill.

BECKY. But I thought you had to learn to take care of Jill.

JILL. Women like us have to learn to give to those who appreciate it instead of to those who expect it.

FRAN. And those cocksucker assholes have been expecting it for centuries.

BECKY. I think you're all fantastic. You are the best women I have ever met. I am *so* glad I came. (*She embraces each of them.*)

FRAN. Thank you, Becky. All right! Now I would like to hear from our "visitor" what she thinks of our rap group so far.

HEIDI. I thought you don't want to be judged.

FRAN. I'm asking you to share. Not to judge.

HEIDI. I think Jill is very generous and I think the girl with the rope bracelet would have been much happier with Donovan.

JILL. (*Laughs.*) Heidi, where do you go to school?

HEIDI. New Haven.

FRAN. Becky, "New Haven" means "Yale" in Eastern egalitarian circles.

HEIDI. I'm in the Art History Graduate Program there. My interest is in images of women from the Renaissance Madonna to the present.

FRAN. A feminist interpretation?

HEIDI. Humanist.

FRAN. Heidi, either you shave your legs or you don't.

HEIDI. I'm afraid I think body hair is in the realm of the personal.

FRAN. What *is* your problem, woman?

HEIDI. I don't really want to share that with you. I'm stingy that way.

SUSAN. My friend Heidi is obsessed with an asshole.

HEIDI. Susie, that's personal.

JILL. "Personal" has kept us apart for so many years.

"Personal" means I know what I'm doing is wrong, but I have so little faith in myself, I'm going to keep it a secret and go right on doing it.

BECKY. Heidi, can I rub your back? Sometimes that helps my mother.

JILL. We shouldn't force her. Maybe Heidi isn't at the same place we are.

HEIDI. I *am* at the same place you are.

FRAN. How are you at the same place we are?

HEIDI. I think all people deserve to fulfill their potential.

FRAN. Yeah. Except for you.

HEIDI. What?

FRAN. Heidi, every woman in this room has been taught that the desires and dreams of her husband, her son, or her boss are much more important than her own. Now the only way to turn that around, is for us, right here, to try to make what *we* want, what we desire, to be as vital to us as it would undoubtedly be to any man. And then we can go out there and really make a difference!

SUSAN. I'm so happy I'm living at this time.

FRAN. Heidi, nothing's going to change until we really start talking to each other.

HEIDI. (*Pause.*) Okay, Fran. I met a guy three years ago at a Eugene McCarthy mixer.

FRAN. Jesus. "Neat and clean for Eugene."

HEIDI. Anyway, we've been seeing each other off and on ever since. He dates a lot of other women, and, uh, I get to see him maybe once every few weeks. He's a teaching fellow at the law school. (*Pause as she catches herself.*) Becky, "The Law School" means "Yale Law School." I'm an Eastern egalitarian asshole from Chicago.

JILL. So big deal.

HEIDI. Thanks.

SUSAN. The point is that Heidi will drop anything, work, a date, even a chance to see me, just to be around this creep.

HEIDI. He is a creep. But he's a charismatic creep.

FRAN. I fuckin' hate charisma.

HEIDI. When I need him, he's aloof. But if I decide to get better and leave him, he's unbelievably attentive.

BECKY. Your asshole sounds just like my asshole.

HEIDI. But you see, Becky, the problem isn't really him. The problem is me. I could make a better choice. I have an old friend, Peter, who I know would be a much better choice. But I keep allowing this guy to account for so much of what I think of myself. I allow him to make me feel valuable. And the bottom line is I know that's wrong. I would tell any friend of mine that's wrong. You either shave your legs or you don't.

FRAN. I like your friend, Susan. She has a way to go, but she's one smart repressed lady.

HEIDI. Becky, I hope our daughters never feel like us. I hope all our daughters feel so fucking worthwhile. Do you promise we can accomplish that much, Fran? Huh? Do you promise? Do you promise?

FRAN. I take it back. I love you, Heidi. (*Fran embraces Heidi.*)

JILL. I love you, Heidi. (*Jill embraces Heidi.*)

BECKY. I love you, Heidi. (*Becky embraces them all.*)

SUSAN. This really has a feeling of completion for me. Full circle. Heidi and I grew up together. We were *girl*friends. But I wanted her to be able to meet my *women* friends because you are all *so* important to me. And Becky, that includes you. You are very important to me now.

JILL. I think we're all just terrific! And I swear that neither snow nor sleet nor Aphrodite's tits could keep me from getting my ass here.

FRAN. (*Fran slaps Jill's hands.*) All right, Jill!

BECKY. (*Slaps Jill's hands.*) All right, Jill!

HEIDI and SUSAN. (*Slaps Jill's hand.*) All right, Jill!

JILL. (*Slaps Heidi's hand.*) All right, Heidi!

BECKY. All right, Heidi!

FRAN. All right, Heidi. (*Fran turns to slap Jill again.*) All right, Jill. (*Jill moves away.*)

JILL. Why don't we all sing a favorite camp song of mine and my children. Okay? Okay. We all get into a circle and join hands. And it goes like this, "Friends, friends, friends, we will always be."

SUSAN. I love you, Jill. (*They all take hands.*)

ALL. (*Singing.*) Friends, friends, friends,
We will always be, (*They all begin to sway.*)

JILL. Whether in hail or in dark stormy weather,
ALL. (*Singing.*) "Whether in hail or in dark stormy weather,"
JILL. Camp Truckahoe will keep us together!
ALL. (*Singing.*) "Camp Truckahoe will . . . (*Fran breaks out of the circle.*)
FRAN. Fuck this shit! (*She puts back on Aretha.*)
ALL. (*Singing along and dancing with each other.*)* "R-E-S-P-E-C-T,
Find out what it means to me.
Sock it to me, a little respect . . .
Sock it to me, a little respect . . .
a little respect . . ."
(*Fran leads the women making a fist salute on "a little respect," each time it is played.*)

END SCENE

SCENE 4

1974, Outside the Chicago Art Institute. It is raining. A man walks across the stage carrying an umbrella and a shopping bag from the Chicago Art Institute. Two women enter with umbrellas and a picket sign "Chicago Women's Art Coalition." Heidi is speaking on a bullhorn. Debbie, standing beside her, is chic and extremely severe in black. They are both holding umbrellas. The women are all chanting "Women in Art!" in front of a banner for an "Age of Napoleon" exhibition.

HEIDI. This museum is publicly funded by our tax dollars. "Our" means both men and women. The weekly attendance at this institution is sixty percent female. The painting and appreciation classes are seventy percent female. Yet this "great" cultural center recognizes and displays only two female artists. And its current offering, The Age of Napoleon, includes not one female artist. (*She turns to Debbie.*) No one's stopping.

---

*Used by permission. See note on page 81.

DEBBIE. (*Takes bullhorn.*) Women artists excluded from this exhibition include Elisabeth Vigee-Lebrun, 1755–1842, painter of over 660 portraits, Marie Benoist, 1768– 1826 . . . (*Peter enters in jeans with a backpack. He, too, carries an umbrella. He is raising his fist as he chants, interrupting Debbie's speech.*)

PETER. No more master-penises. . . . No more master-penises! No more master-penises!

HEIDI. Peter!

DEBBIE. (*Loudly.*) At two o'clock this afternoon, my sisters and I plan to march on the curator's office and demand equal representation for our vision. We urge *you* to join us. (*Peter applauds.*)

PETER. That was terrific. Just great! (*He extends his hand to Debbie.*) Hello, Peter Patrone. (*Debbie doesn't take his hand.*)

DEBBIE. Heidi, I'm afraid some of our group may have gone to the wrong location. Clara, let's go have a look around.

PETER. Right. And I'll beat up any beast who dares go in there with a Rembrandt or a Rubens. (*Debbie and the two other women walk off.*)

HEIDI. Peter, this is *serious!*

PETER. Serious? This is *urgent!* There I was in my lonely intern's cell reminiscing about the three hundred stab wounds I had stitched last night and contemplating taking two Quaaludes for my slight sore throat, when who should be on the pay phone, to say she can't see me because she'll only be in Chicago for four hours, but my innocent youth, my lost love, the lovely and talented Miss Heidi Holland.

HEIDI. Thank you for coming. I think.

PETER. You think? (*He looks around.*) I'm the only one who came!

HEIDI. (*Kisses him.*) You're a good friend.

PETER. *And* I'm a committed and selfless friend! You know what we're missing by being out here? Do you realize that after today, we won't have Dick Nixon to kick around anymore? Bye bye Ehrlichperson and Haldeperson. I'm using nonsexist terminology in honor of your occasion here. (*Heidi looks at him as he closes his umbrella.*) Looks like the gods are smiling on "Women in Art." They want to see more **Grandma Moses.**

HEIDI. Maybe they want to see more Florine Stettheimer.
PETER. I doubt the gods are that esoteric. You look good.
HEIDI. I do?
PETER. A little puffy. A little rhino skin. But you look good.
So are you going to stand here until more women buy paints
and finish a few masterpieces for this sexist, chauvinistic,
creepo institution to exhibit?
HEIDI. You heard Debbie. We're marching on the curator's
office.
PETER. Debbie? Her name is Debbie? Anyone who wears
that much black and silver is not a Debbie! Surely she's a
Deborah. Heidi, you should change your name to Heidarine
or Heidigwyth. Then people will take you seriously. They'd
be flocking here. Not since Woodstock Nation!
HEIDI. You've become cruel in my absence.
PETER. Not cruel. Dyspeptic. I've developed a violent
narcissistic personality disorder.
HEIDI. You have?
PETER. Yes, but don't worry, my darling. According to my
mental health friends, we're heading into a decade of self-
obsession. I am simply at the forefront of the movement.
(*Pause.*) And speaking of the self-obsessed and satisfied, how
is Poopsie?
HEIDI. Scoop. He's in Washington clerking for the Supreme Court.
PETER. Really! He isn't running for president yet! His parents must be ashamed of him. "Harry, Scoop is dead in this
house. Do you hear me? Dead!"
HEIDI. Actually, he and my friend Susan were clerking for
the same judge.
PETER. So you're still in touch with him.
HEIDI. But I'm not involved with him anymore, I just like
sleeping with him.
PETER. What a perky Seventies kind of gal you are! You can
separate sexual needs from emotional dependencies. Heidi,
if you tell me you secrete endorphins when you run, I'm
going straight into the curator's office and demand an all-
armor retrospective.
HEIDI. Don't bother. They're already planning that. Are
you okay?

27

PETER. Actually, I'm afraid I'm feeling sort of distant from you.

HEIDI. Peter, I was writing my dissertation. (*They sit on a nearby bench.*)

PETER. I'm not criticizing you. It's just how I'm feeling. I haven't seen you in eight months.

HEIDI. Peter, you need a girlfriend. I have to find you a girlfriend.

PETER. Please don't.

HEIDI. You've never liked my girlfriends.

PETER. *Women* friends, and I like Fran, the furry physicist from Ann Arbor.

HEIDI. Fran is unavailable. I promise I'll find someone.

PETER. (*Earnestly.*) Heidi, I don't play on your team.

HEIDI. So what? Susan says no man really plays on our team. And no man isn't threatened by our potential. Trust me, you're a lot more secure than most.

PETER. Is Susan the one who used to roll up her skirts with straight pins? She was always giving herself stigmatas in the waist.

HEIDI. She's become a radical shepherdess/counselor.

PETER. Good for her. I've become a liberal homosexual pediatrician.

HEIDI. Well, what I mean is she lives on a woman's health and legal collective in Montana. Susan was clerking for the Supreme Court with Scoop, but, uh, uh . . . she realized she prefers, uh, uh . . .

PETER. Sheep. She realized she prefers sheep. Makes sense. And I prefer Stanley.

HEIDI. Who?

PETER. My friend's name is Stanley Zinc. He's a child psychiatrist from Johns Hopkins. But he's thinking of quitting in order to study with Merce Cunningham. The sad thing is that Stanley is too old to join the company and Miss Merce isn't getting any younger, either. Anyway, I'm thinking of replacing him with a waiter I met last week, we share a mutual distrust of Laura Nyro. I would have told you all this earlier, but I thought we deserved something more intimate than a phone call. So I chose the Chicago Art Institute.

HEIDI. I wish Debbie would get back.

PETER. Why in God's name would you wish that Debbie would get back?

HEIDI. Because you're being impossible.

PETER. How am I being impossible?

HEIDI. You're just being impossible about Susan and her political ideals!

PETER. But I want to celebrate Susan's political ideals!

HEIDI. (*Getting up.*) Fuck off, Peter!

PETER. (*With intensity.*) Heidi, I'm gay, okay? I sleep with Stanley Zinc, M.D. And *my* liberation, *my* pursuit of happiness, and the pursuit of happiness of other men like me is just as politically and socially valid as hanging a couple of God-damned paintings because they were signed by someone named Nancy, Gladys, or Gilda. And that is why I came to see you today. I am demanding your equal time and consideration.

WOMEN. (*From offstage.*) Women in Art! Women in Art!

DEBBIE. Heidi . . .

PETER. Well thank God, Debbie's back and we've got her! (*Debbie walks up to Heidi and Peter with Clara.*)

DEBBIE. I think it's time we made our move. (*She takes out the bullhorn.*) The coalition for Women's Art will be marching on the curator's office. Please join us. (*She begins to march. Clara and Heidi follow and chant with her.*) Women in Art! Women in Art! (*Peter picks up the picket sign and marches with them.*)

PETER. Women in Art!

DEBBIE. (*Stops.*) I find your ironic tone both paternal and caustic. I'm sorry. I can't permit you to join us. This is a women's march.

HEIDI. But I thought that our point was that this is *our* cultural institution. "Our" meaning everybody's. Men and women. Him included.

DEBBIE. Heidi, you know this is a woman's march.

PETER. Heidi, you march. I'll wait for you here.

HEIDI. (*To Debbie.*) I'm sorry, I can't leave my friend.

DEBBIE. God, I despise manipulative men.

PETER. Me, too.

DEBBIE. Suit yourself, Heidi. (*She gets on the bullhorn again.*) Women in Art! Women in Art! (*Debbie marches off.*)

29

PETER. It's too bad she didn't let me march. I know the curator.
HEIDI. Really. What team does he play on?
PETER. Guess.
HEIDI. Oh, Christ.
PETER. Heidi, I know that somewhere you think my world view is small and personal and that yours resonates for generations to come.
HEIDI. I'm going to hit you.
PETER. Oh, c'mon, I dare you. Put up your dukes. (*He takes her hand and punches it against his arm.*) That's for my having distorted sexual politics.
HEIDI. Correct. (*Peter punches himself with her hand again.*)
PETER. And that's because your liberation is better than mine.
HEIDI. Correct again. (*He punches himself with her hand again.*)
PETER. And that's for my decision to treat sick children rather than shepherd radical sheep. (*He hits himself.*) And that's for being paternal. And caustic.
HEIDI. Correct. (*She begins hitting him on her own.*) And that's for being so Goddamned . . .
PETER. Narcissistic? Supercilious?
HEIDI. No. Um . . .
PETER. Sounds like.
HEIDI. Oh, I give up. (*Suddenly she hits him again.*) And that's for liking to sleep with men more than women. (*She hits him again.*) And that's for not being desperately and hopelessly in love with me.
PETER. That hurts!
HEIDI. Suffer.
PETER. (*Pushes her.*) And that's for making me feel guilty.
HEIDI. I did?
PETER. Yes. (*Heidi sighs as if it's all over. Pushes her again.*) And that's for not remembering our tenth anniversary.
HEIDI. We've known each other for ten years?
PETER. Well, nine, but we don't look it. (*He puts his arm around Heidi.*) Heidi, for the first time in my life, I'm optimistic. We just might have very happy lives with enough women's art for everybody. Judy Chicago in the morning,

30

Judy Chicago in the evening, Judy Chicago at dinnertime. Just don't lose your sense of humor or marry that Poop.

HEIDI. Scoop. (*Pause as she looks at him.*) Peter, I'd like to meet Stanley Zinc, doctor-dancer. (*They embrace. However, Peter pulls away as he looks out.*)

PETER. But not imminently, I hope. I left out one thing. Heidi I invited the waiter to meet me here for lunch, and take a deep breath, he's actually shown up.

HEIDI. (*Looking out.*) He's cute.

PETER. He's adorable.

HEIDI. He's okay. (*Mark comes up to them.*)

MARK. Hi.

PETER. Hi. Mark, this is Heidi.

MARK. Hi.

HEIDI. Hi.

PETER. Heidi, Mark. So, what happened?

MARK. It was sad in a way. He was sweating and everything. I wonder if I'll ever want something as much as he wanted to be president.

PETER. Sure you will.

MARK. What?

PETER. Me. You'll want me. (*Peter embraces Mark.*) Everything went great here. I antagonized Debbie and the entire Women in Art delegation, and subsequently Heidi inflicted me with brutal beatings.

MARK. Really?

HEIDI. It's true. But Mark, you can make it up to me.

MARK. I can?

HEIDI. We can still march on the curator's office.

PETER. But what about Debbie? I thought this is a woman's march.

HEIDI. Mark, I am demanding your equal time and consideration. (*She hands him a picket sign.*) Women in Art!

HEIDI and MARK. (*Chanting as they march off.*) Women in Art! Women in Art!

PETER. (*Runs after them.*) Women in Art!

END SCENE

SCENE 5

1977, an anteroom to the ballroom of the Pierre Hotel.
The room is empty except for a few chairs and a table with
flowers and a tray of champagne. Susan and Molly, an
attractive 30-year-old woman, enter. We can hear horah
music from the party next door.

MOLLY. Susan, who are those people?

SUSAN. Well, Molly, Heidi's my oldest friend, Peter's a
doctor, the bride I've never met before and the groom is a
prick.

MOLLY. Susie, I have a feeling we're not in Montana anymore. *(Peter and Heidi enter. Peter in a suit, Heidi in a lovely
dress.)*

PETER. "Do you, Scoop Rosenbaum, take Lisa Friedlander
to be your bride?" "Well, I feel ambivalent about her. But I
am blocked emotionally and she went to good schools, comes
from a very good family and is not particularly threatening.
So, yay, I do. Anyway, it's time for me to get married." "And
do you, Lisa, take Scoop?" *(He speaks her answer with Lisa's
Southern accent.)* "Rabbi, ever since I was a little girl I've been
wanting to matriculate with an M.R.S. degree. I idolize
Scoop because he is as brilliant and will be as rich as my daddy
whom I also idolize. And I am a slight masochist. Although I
do come from the best Jewish family in Memphis. So, yes,
Rabbi, I do take Scoop." "And now under the eyes of God
and The Pierre Hotel, I pronounce you man and M.R.S.
degree."

SUSAN. I never knew the deity and the Pierre had a package
deal.

PETER. Oh sure. And for a $10,000 donation, the Holy-Be-
He will throw in table flowers and a four-piece combo.
Honestly, I've never seen a less romantic-looking bride.

HEIDI. Peter, shhh. She looked very tasteful.

PETER. She looked like Woody Woodpecker.

SUSAN. And those bridesmaids looked like flying
buttresses!

MOLLY. *(Giggling.)* I'm sure she's a very nice person.

PETER. You're right, Molly. I'm sure she's a very nice person, too.

SUSAN. I'm surprised he married someone so bland.
PETER. Susan, do your sisters know you are capable of calling another woman bland!
HEIDI. We should go in there and shake hands.
SUSAN. What is with you today?
HEIDI. I'd marry her.
MOLLY. (Still giggling.) She had no meat on her.
PETER. I love you, Molly.
HEIDI. They'll be very happy. She's perfect for Scoop. (Scoop enters. Heidi doesn't notice him at first.)
SCOOP. How do you know?
MOLLY. Are you the groom?
SCOOP. Yes.
MOLLY. (Goes up to Scoop.) I heard you're a prick.
SUSAN. (Waves.) Hi, Scoop.
SCOOP. (Waves.) Hi, Susan.
SUSAN. Scoop, this is my friend Molly McBride from the Montana Women's Health and Legal Collective. (Scoop shakes her hand.)
SCOOP. Any sister shepherdess is always a pleasure. (To Peter.) And you must be the pediatrician.
PETER. (Shakes Scoop's hand.) Mazel tov.
SCOOP. Heidella speaks so fondly of you. I can't understand why she never introduced us.
PETER. Heidella, why have you kept us apart? (Heidi glowers at Peter.)
SCOOP. I wish you would all go into the reception. You're the most interesting people here.
HEIDI. I thought Jonas Salk was here.
MOLLY. I thought Burt Lance was here.
PETER. I thought David Cassidy was here.
SCOOP. They're all here. I told you you're the most interesting people at this party. Please help me out. Without you I'm just another junior associate at Sullivan Cromwell at another Pierre wedding. It's beyond depressing.
MOLLY. Well, heck, I'll go in. I always like a good party.
SCOOP. (His arm around Molly.) Molly, I think our country is fortunate that Felix Frankfurter didn't meet such an appealing alternative lifestyle during his formative days. You know, I clerked with Susan. She could have been brilliant.
HEIDI. Susan is brilliant.

33

SCOOP. Brilliance is irrelevant in Montana.

PETER. (*Gets up.*) Well, I think our continued presence here is up to Heidi.

SUSAN. Heidi's not saying anything. That means she wants to stay. (*She grabs Molly.*) C'mon, Mol, we're gonna horah like nobody's ever horahed. Maybe we can convince the bride to dump him and become irrelevant in Montana. (*Susan and Molly exit.*)

HEIDI. Susan's angry with me.

SCOOP. Susan's crazy.

HEIDI. No she's not.

SCOOP. She's a fanatic and she's crazy. Do you know she was voted one of the ten most attractive "new" women in Washington? I could have been interested in Susan.

PETER. Does Susan know this? She might drown Molly.

HEIDI. Susan's not involved with Molly.

SCOOP. You mean she's like our president? Only in her heart she lusts for other women.

HEIDI. Susan is very committed. She's thinking of going to business school so the collective can become self-sufficient.

SCOOP. She'll be on Wall Street in two years. Believe me. (*Peter is staring at Scoop. Scoop looks up at him.*)

PETER. Are you in love?

SCOOP. Excuse me?

PETER. I like to think that when two people our age get married, they are in love. (*Heidi takes Peter's arm.*)

HEIDI. Peter's very romantic.

SCOOP. I see. Are you an item now?

HEIDI. No.

PETER. (*Louder.*) Yes.

SCOOP. Makes sense. Lisa marries a nice Jewish lawyer, Heidi marries a warm Italian pediatrician. It's all interchangeable, isn't it? To answer your question, "Am I in love?", sure, why not. (*Scoop lights a cigar.*)

HEIDI. (*Squeezes Peter's hand.*) Why not. (*Lisa, deliberately classy, enters. She speaks with a very slight Southern accent.*)

LISA. Sweetie, they're about to play our first dance. (*Lisa and Scoop kiss.*)

SCOOP. Sweetie, this is Peter Patrone and his fiancee, Heidi. Peter is a pediatrics resident at Bellevue.

34

LISA. Hey there. How nice to see you.

SCOOP. I was just telling Peter that we're hoping for a large family.

PETER. Not common these days.

LISA. I've always known I wanted to be a mom. I guess that's pretty embarrassing.

PETER. (*To Heidi.*) Sweetie, do you think that's embarrassing?

HEIDI. No, sweetie, of course not. Not at all.

LISA. Well, I am going to keep up my illustration work.

SCOOP. Lisa's books are very popular.

PETER. Wait a second. Are you Lisa Friedlander, the illustrator of *King, Ginger, the Lion*?

LISA. You know *King Ginger*?

PETER. The best medical text in this country is *King Ginger Goes to the Hospital*.

SCOOP. (*Puts his arm around Lisa.*) She's terrific. Isn't she?

PETER. There'll be a riot in my waiting room if you stop working.

SCOOP. Well, we'll see.

LISA. Sweetie, don't be such a little piggy. Dr. Patrone, would you join me for my first dance? Obviously, my husband has decided to be antisocial at his own wedding.

SCOOP. I'm being what?

LISA. Heidi, don't you hate that we can only get a reaction out of our men when they feel competitive? But maybe that's why it's so much fun to push them around. (*She winks at Heidi and turns back to Scoop.*) Oh, and sweetie, one more thing. There are two women I don't recognize waltzing around the dance floor together. Aunt Florence thinks they're interlopers. (*She takes Peter's arm.*) Shake your booties doctor. (*They begin to exit as Ballroom music is heard.*)

PETER. (*Turns back, softly.*) See ya.

HEIDI. Did she just say "Shake your booties, doctor?"

SCOOP. (*Sits down and sighs in mock despair.*) Oh God, I'm so unhappy!

HEIDI. She must be very talented.

SCOOP. Why did you let me do this?

HEIDI. Me! What do you mean, why did *I* let you? I had nothing to do with this.

SCOOP. Yes, you did. Are you marrying this doctor?
HEIDI. Maybe.
SCOOP. Seems like a nice enough guy.
HEIDI. He's a wonderful guy. He's also gay. Anyway, I'm seeing someone. Sort of living with someone.
SCOOP. (*With accent.*) So vhere is he? I vant to have a look.
HEIDI. I didn't vant you to meet him. I didn't vant you to have a look.
SCOOP Is he quality goods?
HEIDI. He's an editor.
SCOOP. An editor?
HEIDI. I met him through work. I'm writing a book of essays.
SCOOP. Academic?
HEIDI. Sort of.
SCOOP. Art history?
HEIDI. Sort of.
SCOOP. Sounds like there's miniseries potential here.
HEIDI. It's called *And the Light Floods in From the Left and Other Over-Commitments.* Essays on art and women.
SCOOP. (*Smiles.*) Sort of Marcusian. (*Heidi, increasingly nervous, begins shredding a cocktail napkin.*)
HEIDI. Well, actually, it's sort of humorous. Well, sort of social observation. I mean, it's sort of a point of view. (*Scoop takes her hand.*)
SCOOP. Heidella, don't shred the napkin.
HEIDI. I'm sorry.
SCOOP. Aunt Florence will never recover from who's been at the Pierre today. (*Heidi bends down and starts picking up the shredded napkin.*) I didn't ask you to clean the room. I just told you not to shred. Maybe you should spend some time on that collective in Montana. Liberate yourself. So, who's this editor?
HEIDI. I don't have to answer these questions.
SCOOP. Heidi, I'm a lawyer and I'm about to be a journalist again. So, yes, actually it'll be easier if you do answer these questions.
HEIDI. What do you mean you're about to be a journalist again?
SCOOP. I'm starting a magazine.

36

HEIDI. What magazine?

SCOOP. I answered your question, now you have to answer mine. Who's this editor?

HEIDI. Christ . . .

SCOOP. I'm just trying to have a friendly conversation. I'm concerned about you. I care about you. Where did he go to school?

HEIDI. Trinity.

SCOOP. Trinity? Trinity what? Trinity, Cambridge? Trinity, Hartford? Trinity, the Lower School?

HEIDI. Trinity, Hartford.

SCOOP. (*Aghast.*) You're sort of living with an editor who went to Trinity College, Hartford!

HEIDI. You've certainly come a long way from *The Liberated Earth News.*

SCOOP. Did I say anything? I didn't say anything. Where does he edit?

HEIDI. *Hustler.*

SCOOP. He should only be half as creative as an editor at *Hustler* and an eighth as well endowed.

HEIDI. You don't even know him.

SCOOP. Yes I do. Where does he edit, Knopf?

HEIDI. Do you interrogate Lisa like this?

SCOOP. No. I know who Lisa sort of lives with. Simon & Schuster?

HEIDI. No.

SCOOP. Harper and Row?

HEIDI. I don't know.

SCOOP. Harper and Row. It's Harper and Row. Way to go, Rosenbaum.

HEIDI. I hate this. I really hate this.

SCOOP. No, you don't. Or you wouldn't have come.

HEIDI. Peter wanted to meet you. That's why we came. He said if I witnessed your ritual it would put an end to an era. And Susan, for some insane reason, Susan wanted to come, too.

SCOOP. Maybe she's got a thing for Burt Lance.

HEIDI. No, Molly wanted to see New York. This all is irrelevant. I'm thinking of writing my book in England. I applied for a Fulbright.

37

SCOOP. (*Surprised.*) Heidella, if you haven't won this partic- ular round, it doesn't mean you have to drop completely out of the match.

HEIDI. You still use lousy construction.

SCOOP. Yes, I do. And that's what makes me so much more interesting than the editor.

HEIDI. Fuck you.

SCOOP. You still use foul language.

HEIDI. You don't?

SCOOP. My wife doesn't care for it.

HEIDI. Well, clearly she's quality goods. (*Pause.*)

SCOOP. You really don't understand, do you?

HEIDI. I think I do.

SCOOP. No, you don't. But I can explain. Let's say we mar- ried and I asked you to devote the, say, next ten years of your life to me. To making me a home and a family and a life so secure that I could with some confidence go out into the world each day and attempt to get an "A." You'd say "No." You'd say "Why can't we be partners? Why can't we both go out into the world and get an 'A'?" And you'd be absolutely valid and correct.

HEIDI. But Lisa . . .

SCOOP. "Do I love her," as your nice friend asked me? She's the best that I can do. Is she an "A+" like you? No. But I don't want to come home to an "A+." "A−" maybe, but not "A+."

HEIDI. Scoop, we're out of school. We're in life. You don't need to grade everything.

SCOOP. I'm sorry, Heidella. But I couldn't dangle you any- more. And that's why I got married today. So.

HEIDI. So. So now it's all my fault.

SCOOP. Sure it is. You want other things in life than I do.

HEIDI. Really? Like what?

SCOOP. Self-fulfillment. Self-determination. Self-exag- geration.

HEIDI. That's exactly what you want.

SCOOP. Right. Then you'd be competing with me. (*Pause.*)

HEIDI. (*Softly.*) Scoop . . .

SCOOP. What?

HEIDI. Forget it. (*He puts his arm around her tenderly.*)

38

SCOOP. What, baby?

HEIDI. I.

SCOOP. It's either/or.

HEIDI. That is simply not true.

SCOOP. You don't like the grades. Fuck the grades. Let's try numbers.

HEIDI. I thought you don't use foul language.

SCOOP. I don't. Unless it's helpful. On a scale from one to ten, if you aim for six and get six, everything will work out nicely. But if you aim for ten in all things and get six, you're going to be very disappointed. And unfortunately, that's why you "quality time" girls are going to be one generation of disappointed women. Interesting, exemplary, even sexy, but basically unhappy. The ones who open doors usually are.

HEIDI. But you're willing to settle for a secure six?

SCOOP. I've got more important things to worry about.

HEIDI. Your magazine?

SCOOP. Just things. It's all home cooking in the crock pot you bought us. By the way, I was hurt by that. It's not a very personal gift.

HEIDI. I'll send a Mister Coffee. (*She extends her hand.*) Bye, Scoop. Congratulations.

SCOOP. (*Holds her hand.*) I'm sorry I disappointed you.

HEIDI. I don't give grades.

SCOOP. I told you in New Hampshire you'd be the one this would all make such a difference to.

HEIDI. I've yet to torch lingerie.

SCOOP. We're talking life choices.

HEIDI. I haven't made them yet.

SCOOP. Yes you have, or we'd be getting married today.

HEIDI. Scoop, we'd never break a glass at the Pierre.

SCOOP. I didn't marry Lisa because she's Jewish.

HEIDI. No, you married her because she's blandish.

SCOOP. I never meant to hurt you.

HEIDI. (*Averting eyes.*) I gotta go or Peter will abandon me for a waiter. He's into waiters.

SCOOP. Really, but he's a well-educated man. He went to Williams.

HEIDI. Williams men like to come home to a well-set table, too.

SCOOP. (*Laughs.*) Vicious dumpling. (*There is a drum roll and then the voice of the master of ceremonies next door is heard.*)
VOICEOVER. Ladies and gentlemen, Lisa and Scoop have requested this recording of their favorite song. (*"You Send Me" begins to play.* She motions for him to go. He starts to leave. They look at each other.*)
SCOOP. Are you guarding the chips? (*They simultaneously move towards each other and kiss. They are suddenly slow dancing. Scoop laughs.*) The editor of *Hustler*? (*They continue to dance as the music plays.*)
HEIDI. Sam Cooke.
SCOOP. "A+" content.
HEIDI. "A+" form.
SCOOP. I love you, Heidi. I'll always love you.
HEIDI. (*Shakes her head slightly.*) Oh, please . . . (*She puts her head on his shoulder. He holds her tightly as he sings.*)
SCOOP. "Darling, you send me.
Honest you do.
Honest you do."*
(*Lights fade as they slow dance.*)

END OF ACT ONE

---

*Used by permission. See note on page 81.

ACT TWO

PROLOGUE

1989, lecture hall, Columbia University.

HEIDI. Lilla Cabot Perry, 1848–1933, was, along with the better known Mary Cassatt and Berthe Morisot, a major influence in American Impressionism. Her painting "Lady With a Bowl of Violets." (*The wrong slide has come onto the screen. Heidi pauses.*) Lilla went through a little known hostility period . . . actually the painting you're looking at is "Judith Beheading Holofernes" by Artemisia Gentileschi. Please bear with me. My T.A. is taking the law boards today. (*The correct slide comes on.*)

Thank you. "Lady with a Bowl of Violets." Notice how the tones move from cool blues and violets to warmer oranges lighting up the collar of the rather flimsy negligee. Change flimsy to flouncy. But Lilla cops out when she gets to the head. Suddenly, we're back to traditional portraiture with the lines completely delineated.

The painting I prefer, is "Lady in Evening Dress" painted in 1911. Closer to her mentor Monet, Lilla here is willing to lose her edges in favor of paint and light. Go Lilla! Now let's compare for a moment Cabot's "Lady" with Lily Martin Spencer's fading rose. There is something uniquely female about these paintings. And I'm not referring to their lovely qualities, delicate techniques, or overall charm. Oh, please! What strikes me is both ladies seem slightly removed from the occasions at hand. They appear to watch closely and ease the way for the others to join in. I suppose it's really not unlike being an art historian. In other words, being neither the painter, nor the casual observer, but a highly informed spectator.

END OF PROLOGUE

SCENE 1

1980, Scoop and Lisa's apartment. A pile of opened boxes and paper wrapping are on the coffee table. Lisa, *very pregnant, Betsy, also very pregnant, around 35, Denise, 24, in a suit, tie and sneakers, and Susan, with a new look in pants, heels, and silk blouse. Betsy is making a hat out of wrapping paper. A song like "Imagine" is playing in the background.* Lisa pulls out a tiny robe, tiny gown and slippers from a gift box.*

LISA. *(Holding up a gown.)* Ooooooooh that's adorable!

DENISE. It's a robe and a nighty. Lisa, that's the cutest thing I've ever seen.

SUSAN. Look at those tiny slippers. How could anything be so tiny?

BETSY. Shhhh! Let's listen to this. *(They listen to song.)*

SUSAN. I don't think I can listen to much more of this or I'll start crying again. *(She takes the record off.)*

LISA. Denise let's put on a different song. Something snappy from when the Beatles were all together. Like "Rocky Raccoon."

SUSAN. "It's been a Hard Days Night" was on my stereo the first time I slept with my high school/first year of college boyfriend. His signature was twisting and smoking simultaneously.

LISA. "Here Comes the Sun" was on my stereo the first time I slept with Scoop.

BETSY. Really!

LISA. What can I say. I've always been an oddly well ad-justed and cheerful person.

DENISE. You're just normal.

LISA. Thank you, Denise. You're a sweet sister. *(Doorbell.)*

SUSAN. That must be Heidi.

LISA. Cha-cha will get it.

SUSAN. I told Heidi to come right over after the park.

BETSY. I can't believe people actually went to that.

SUSAN. She was curious. And I think she was really upset.

BETSY. Well, we were all upset! But the thought of mass weeping with Yoko in Central Park . . .

HEIDI. *(Heidi enters.)* Hi Hi. Sorry I'm late. Lisa, lovely to see you again.

---

*See Special Note on copyright page.

42

SUSAN. See you can tell she's been living in England. She says "lovely" every chance she gets. Heidi, this is Lisa's sister Denise. And you know Betsy.
BETSY. (*She shakes Heidi's hand.*) Sure, we go back to my *Liberated Earth News* days.
LISA. Betsy's now managing editor of Scoop's magazine.
HEIDI. I saw a copy of *Boomer* in London. Looks terrific.
BETSY. Lisa, let's get this woman some wine. (*Lisa gives Heidi wine and offers to Susan.*) Susie, how 'bout some more.
SUSAN. I can't. I've been living on rabbit food for a month now and I'm still a truck.
LISA. Scoop says that you're the most handsome woman he knows.
SUSAN. Handsome means truck.
BETSY. My sweet husband says men prefer a woman with a little thigh.
SUSAN. Well, all right. Lisa, open another gift!
BETSY. Definitely time for another gift. (*Denise hands Lisa another present.*)
LISA. Denise, who was that nighty from?
DENISE. (*Denise looks at a list she's been keeping.*) Patti Bennett.
LISA. Why did Patti leave so early?
BETSY. Patti's daughter didn't get into kindergarten at Ethical Culture and now Charlie's making the entire family go into therapy.
HEIDI. You're joking.
BETSY. Today's their first session.
HEIDI. Really.
BETSY. (*Patting her stomach.*) Sure. I've already signed this one up for a cram course for the E.R.B's.
HEIDI. What's that?
BETSY. They're the S.A.T.'s for nursery school.
HEIDI. And they have cram courses. I really have been living out of the country for too long.
LISA. What's Charlie Bennett's daughter's name?
SUSAN. Jennifer.
LISA. Oh, I hate those "J" names. So common. Scoop wants to call this one Maggie or Pierre in honor of his French Canadian roots. (*She looks at card on the next present.*) This one's from Susie!!

43

SUSAN. This one's a thank you present. With Heidi gone, I couldn't have survived moving here without you and Scoop.
DENISE. Where did you live before?
SUSAN. Montana.
DENISE. You lived in Montana?
SUSAN. Before business school I belonged to a Woman's Health and Legal Collective there.
DENISE. You mean like a dude ranch?
SUSAN. Like a feminist dude ranch.
HEIDI. Denise, have you never heard of a woman's collective?
DENISE. Oh, sure I have. I took women's studies at Brown. (*Lisa pulls a leopard snuggly out of the box.*) Oh, that is fabulous!!
LISA. I've never seen a leopard snuggly!!
BETSY. That's hysterical!!
DENISE. I love it! Don't you love it, Heidi! Susan, this gift could only have come from you. I mean it's just so Susan!
SUSAN. That's me! Wild, practical, and fifty percent rayon.
LISA. Thank you. Susie, what did you decide to do about L.A.?
DENISE. Yeah?
SUSAN. I've accepted the position.
BETSY. What position?
SUSAN. I just took a job in L.A. as executive V.P. for a new production company. They wanted someone with a feminist and business background. Targeting films for the 25-to-29-year-old female audience.
BETSY. Lisa, you know some fantastic women. I tell you, this is one power shower!! (*She toasts.*)
DENISE. (*Toasting.*) Here! Here!
SUSAN. Heidi, I know some of those Hollywood people can be pretty dreadful, but if I don't do it, someone who cares a lot less will.
DENISE. I'd move to L.A. in a minute. (*Denise picks up the last box.*) This one has no card.
HEIDI. Oh, oh that's mine!
LISA. Heidi, Scoop was so excited when I told him Susie invited you here today. He's really sorry to have missed you. He had to go up to Princeton for one of those "looking

forward to the eighties, looking back on the seventies" panels.

BETSY. I should have been on that panel. I smoked and drank things with Scoop on the *Liberated Earth News* in 1969 that could make Three Mile Island look like a health spa.

SUSAN. The topic was something like "What does the election of Ronald Reagan mean to the Greening of America?"

HEIDI. Good question.

DENISE. Everyone says he's the best for the economy. (*The other women all look at Denise.*) Cheer up, kids. The 80's are going to be great.

SUSAN. Heidi, are you okay?

HEIDI. Oh, I'm fine. I just had to get up early to meet Peter at the park.

LISA. Heidi, you should grab him. Maybe he'll change. He obviously loves children.

BETSY. Who's this?

LISA. Peter Patrone. Betsy, you know him. *Boomer* did that cover story on him.

BETSY. Oh, "The Best Pediatrician in New York Under Forty."

DENISE. Is he married?

HEIDI. Well, actually, he did finally break up last month with Stanley.

DENISE. Oh, fuck piss!

LISA. Denise!

DENISE. I'm sorry, but there's absolutely no one. And once my career's in place, I definitely want to have my children before I'm thirty. I mean, isn't that what you guys fought for? So we could "have it all." I mean, don't you want to have a family, Heidi?

HEIDI. Yes, I hope so.

LISA. You have plenty of time, Heidi.

SUSAN. Well, you almost got married in England.

BETSY. But what happened?

HEIDI. Well, I got this job at Columbia and he wanted to stay in London.

BETSY. It's just so unfair. My single women friends are such fabulous attractive people! I wish I knew someone for each of you. But Denise is right. There's absolutely no one. (*Lisa*

45

opens the box. She pulls a furry funny stuffed animal out of the box. It is half elephant, half hippo.)

LISA. Heidi, this is *so* sweet!

BETSY. Look at its little head.

SUSAN. (*She grabs it.*) I want to marry this.

DENISE. I can't believe it. I mean this could only have come from you.

HEIDI. I know. It's just so "Heidi"! Actually, it's a Heffalump. Half elephant. Half Hippo. From a Winnie the Pooh story.

BETSY. I'm a Heffalump. Half elephant, half lump. Now that I've drunk enough to deliver a nasal passage. I have to tell you, Heidi, that I loved *And The Light Floods In From The Left.*

DENISE. You know, a lot of people are talking about your book. Heidi, this T.V. show I'm like a production assistant at, "Hello New York," is devoting a series to "Women in the 80's." What we've gained. What we've lost. And April, our host, was very excited when I told her that I'd be seeing you today. (*The phone rings.*) We thought we could do something on you and Women in Art. Excuse me. (*Denise rushes out of room.*)

LISA. My little sister is so up and positive. I just get so tired sometimes.

BETSY. I get tired all the time. Lisa, why doesn't Denise have a Southern accent?

SUSAN. Maybe she liberated it during women's studies at Brown.

LISA. My little sister is the "New South." (*Denise reenters.*)

DENISE. Lis, it's your husband. He's still at Princeton.

LISA. Please don't say anything juicy 'till I get back. (*Lisa exits. Pause.*)

BETSY. (*Quietly.*) I honestly don't think she knows.

DENISE. Oh, Lisa knows. She was being really cheerful. That means she knows.

BETSY. Honestly, you should see his little friend. She's a graphics assistant on the magazine. Runs around New York in leather miniskirts and fishnet stockings. And she's not very bright. She's like that entire generation. Except for you, Denise. She has opinions on everything and she's done noth-

46

ing. Oh, I'm sorry, Heidi. It's just someone we both don't care for very much.

HEIDI. You mean the woman Scoop's seeing?

SUSAN. What?

HEIDI. Susie, this morning I was with the best pediatrician under forty at the John Lennon memorial in Central Park, and Scoop was not at Princeton. Scoop and the graphics assistant were also in Central Park.

SUSAN. Maybe it wasn't him.

HEIDI. Oh, it was him. He embraced me. Shook hands with Peter. He said it was very important we were all there. He said this was for our generation.

BETSY. So you met her?

HEIDI. Yes. Fishnet stockings, has opinions.

SUSAN. Was he mortified?

HEIDI. No. He told me my book was "A—" inspiration, "B" followthrough.

SUSAN. That's all.

HEIDI. He apologized. He said he didn't want to be rude, but he was too moved to speak. Then he cried, she cried, and they walked away.

BETSY. Well, I'm certainly touched.

SUSAN. Oh, she's just horrible!

BETSY. Susie, what about him!

HEIDI. I wasn't surprised really. I wasn't impressed. But I wasn't surprised.

BETSY. I like men. But they're really not very nice. (*Lisa reenters the room.*)

LISA. Who's not very nice?

DENISE. Oh, this guy who works at *Boomer* that someone was going to fix me up with.

LISA. But who were you huddling about when I came in?

BETSY. You.

LISA. Me?

BETSY. We finished your hat. (*She gives Lisa the hat made from wrapping paper and ribbon. Betsy begins to tie it on her.*)

LISA. What? Oh, gosh. I wish you all knew how much I appreciate this. Betsy's right, you are fantastic women. (*She begins to cry.*) Oh, oh, yuck, I'm sorry. Scoop says I'm like an emotional bumper car.

SUSAN. That's okay, honey.
LISA. Honest to God. I love women. I really do. (*She gathers herself.*) Okay, end of Lisa's dumb episode. Betsy, let's continue our tribute.
BETSY. (*Puts her arm around Lisa.*) Lisa, are you . . . ?
LISA. (*Smiles.*) Shake your booties, Betsy. (*Betsy puts the record back on.*)
SUSAN. Wait! First a farewell to John. (*She lifts her glass.*) To John!
ALL. To John!
HEIDI. And Ringo, and Paul, and George!
LISA. Forever!
ALL. And Ringo, and Paul, and George, forever! (*They toast each other as the song plays and the lights fade.*)

END SCENE

SCENE 2

1982, a T.V. studio. Steve, a studio attendant, is onstage calling light cues.

STEVE. Give me 189. Let's restore it. (*We hear "Steve to the control room, please. Steve to the control room," over the loudspeaker as Scoop and Peter enter.*)
PETER. I'm ready for my close up, Mr. DeMille.
SCOOP. I think it's a terrific idea of Lisa's sister to have us all on the show together. Too bad Susie couldn't make it.
PETER. Who's Susie?
SCOOP. Susan.
PETER. Oh, the radical shepherdess.
SCOOP. Now the studio vice president.
STEVE. (*Putting "mic" on Peter.*) Okay, you're all set. (*Denise enters with Heidi. Denise is very pregnant.*)
DENISE. Hi, guys.
HEIDI. Hi, Scoop.
SCOOP. (*Embraces her.*) Hi, Heidi, great to see you.
STEVE. Where do you want her?
DENISE. In the middle. Thanks for coming, guys, we're all very excited about this segment. You're a real cross section.

SCOOP. Peter, this is Lisa's sister Denise.

PETER. Oh, hi!

DENISE. Lisa says I have to use you for this one. She says you're the best. You're there and Scoop you're there.

HEIDI. Congratulations on the new baby.

SCOOP. Number two. Way to go, Rosenbaum.

DENISE. (*Quiets them.*) Okay. Okay. (*Looking at her clipboard.*) Some of the topics April wants to cover today are the sixties, social conscience, relationships, Reaganomics, money, careers, approaching the big 4-0, Scoop: opinions, trends, Heidi: women in art, the death of the ERA, your book, Peter: the new medicine, kids today, and April says the further out you can take your sexuality, the better. Our audiences enjoy a little controversy with their coffee. Okay?

PETER. (*Stunned.*) What?

VOICEOVER. Ten seconds please. (*April enters. The show theme plays.*)

APRIL. Hi guys.

ATTENDANT. Five, four, three . . . (*Hand signals two, one, go to April.*)

APRIL. If you've just joined us, I'm April Lambert, and this is "Hello New York." We're speaking today with members of the baby boom generation. The kids who grew up in the fifties, protested in the sixties, were the "me's" of the seventies, and the parents of the eighties. Here with us today are Scoop Rosenbaum, editor of the very successful and influential *Boomer* magazine, Heidi Holland, author of *And the Light Floods In from the Left* and director of Womanzart. Is that pronounced like Mozart?

HEIDI. Well, actually it's Woman's Art.

APRIL. Excuse me, Woman's Art. A group dedicated to the recognition of American women artists, and Dr. Peter Patrone, who is, according to *Boomer* magazine, for two years now the leading pediatrician in New York under forty. Boy, I'm impressed! Good morning to all of you.

PETER. Good morning, April. First of all, let me say I think a standard for success for our generation is being able to say "Good morning, April!" in person. I have to say I am very grateful for this opportunity, April.

APRIL. Thank you. Scoop, you've been an editor since

1967, when you started *The Liberated Earth News.* You've certainly had a lot of success since then.

SCOOP. April, I'm just a simple newspaper man.

APRIL. Do you think the values of our generation have changed significantly since the sixties?

SCOOP. April, I think we're a generation that is still idealistic, and idealists wonder what they're going to do when they grow up. I'll be wondering 'till I'm eighty.

APRIL. I once heard the same thing about Bertrand Russell. Heidi, how do you feel about that?

HEIDI. I don't really know much about Bertrand Russell.

APRIL. Peter, you're a doctor. You work with children. Do you see yourself as a grown-up?

PETER. Yes. I'm very old and very wise.

APRIL. We were known as the baby boom generation. Do you think starting our own families now makes a difference in accepting our place as adults?

SCOOP. April, I have two children, Maggie and Pierre. My wife and I were into Canadians at the time. Whether they make me an official adult or not, I really don't know. But having my own family has certainly pulled me out of any "Me Generation" residue. The future is about my kids, not me.

APRIL. Lucky kids. Heidi, there's a lot of talk these days about superwomen. Are you a superwoman?

HEIDI. Oh gosh, no. You have to keep too many lists to be a superwoman.

APRIL. I love lists. You should see my refrigerator.

PETER. Do you keep lists *in* your refrigerator?

APRIL. (*Laughs.*) Well, they can't say we don't have a sense of humor. Heidi, a lot of women are beginning to feel you can't have it all. Do you think it's time to compromise?

HEIDI. Well, I think that depends on . . .

SCOOP. (*Cuts her off.*) Can I interrupt and say that I think if we're asking women to compromise, then we also have to ask men to compromise. This year, my wife Lisa won the Widener Prize for her illustrations of *King Ginger Goes to Summer Camp.* I'm every bit as proud of that as I am of *Boomer* magazine.

APRIL. But Scoop, everyone isn't as capable as Lisa. For instance, a lot of my single women friends are panicked now about their biological clocks winding down. Do you find that's true, Heidi?

HEIDI. If you look . . .

PETER. (*Cuts her off.*) April, can I still call you "April"?

APRIL. You have the sweetest face. Can we get a close-up of this face?

PETER. April, I run one of the largest pediatric units in this country. And I am here to tell you that most women can have healthy and happy children 'till well after forty-two.

APRIL. Well, my friends will certainly be happy to hear that. Peter, so far you've chosen not to have children.

PETER. (*After a pause.*) I think, April, what distinguishes our generation from the previous one is our belief that any individual has a right to pursue his or her particular lifestyle. In other words, say you want to dress up as a Tylenol capsule to host "Hello New York" tomorrow . . . (*In outrageous mock-camp.*) I'd say there's no need, but why not? Go for it! (*She looks at him and back at her card.*)

APRIL. (*To Heidi.*) So what's next? After the kids and the country house? Once we're settled, Heidi, do you think we'll see a resurgence of a social conscience?

HEIDI. Uh . . .

PETER. (*Cuts her off.*) Yes, Betsy Bloomingdale will be at the barricades.

APRIL. Heidi . . .

SCOOP. (*Jumps in.*) There's a line in a Ferlinghetti poem. "And I am awaiting the rebirth of Wonder." I think we're all awaiting a rebirth of wonder.

PETER. What does that mean exactly? I wonder.

APRIL. (*Sharp.*) I'm afraid we only have a minute left. Scoop, *Boomer* magazine was an immediate success. Something very rare in the magazine business. Why?

SCOOP. Well, as you've seen this morning, we're serious people with a sense of humor. We're not young professionals, and we're not old lefties or righties. We're unique. We're powerful, but not bullies. We're rich, but not ostentatious. We're parents, but we're not parental. And I think we had the left magazines in college, we had the music magazines in the seventies, and now we deserve what I call a "power" magazine in the eighties. We're opinion and trendsetters, and I hope *Boomer* is our chronicle.

APRIL. It certainly looks like it's heading in that direction. The baby boom generation, are we all grown up now? Well, we're rich, powerful, famous, and even parents. But who knows what we'd do if Peter Pan came through our bedroom windows. (*Peter mouths "I do."*) Thank you, Scoop Rosenbaum, editor of *Boomer* magazine, Heidi Holland, essayist, curator, feminist, and Dr. Peter Patrone, chief of Pediatrics at New York Hospital.

PETER. Thank you, April. Goodbye, New York.

APRIL. Bert will be back with the weather in just a moment. (*The music returns. They sit still till lights go out. April gets up immediately.*) A Tylenol capsule! You're too much. (*Denise returns.*)

DENISE. April, Senator Moore's wife is here with "Divorced Senate Wives modelling coats for Spring" in studio three. (*To Heidi, Peter, Scoop.*) Fabulous segment, guys. (*To Peter.*) You. The Senate wives loved Betsy Bloomingdale.

APRIL. Denise, would you go get my book? (*Denise exits. April turns to them and begins shaking hands.*) That was tremendous, guys. Thanks for coming. Sorry I have to rush off, but take your time.

SCOOP. April, Lisa and I are meeting up with a few people at Le Cirque for lunch later. Why don't you and David join us?

APRIL. Who else will be there?

PETER. Oh, the regulars. Farrah and Ryan, Noam Chomsky, Bishop Tutu, Bernie Bosanquet.

APRIL. Who?

SCOOP. Bernard Bosanquet. Nineteenth-century British political philosopher.

APRIL. So he's not coming?

SCOOP. No. Peter's being cynical again.

APRIL. That face is so sweet and that mind is so savage.

PETER. Oh, I like savage. Say that again.

SCOOP. Actually, my friend Paul's in town. Heidi, you met Paul in Manchester years ago.

PETER. Is "Paul" Paul Newman?

APRIL. We'll come.

VOICEOVER. April to Studio Three.

APRIL. Scoop, wait here. I'll be right back. (*April exits.*)
PETER. (*Declaiming.*)
"Wan that Aprille with her shoures scote,
The droghte of human stupidity hath perced to the roote."
SCOOP. April Lambert is irrelevant. David Lambert owns 60 buildings in Manhattan. Peter, you were hilarious. I enjoyed myself immensely.
PETER. Of course you did. You won.
SCOOP. I'd say if anyone won it was Heidi. She didn't feel compelled to be cynical like you or go out for another "A" like me.
PETER. No, she didn't say anything.
HEIDI. How could I say anything when both of you were so eager and willing to say it for me? You two should become regulars on the show, the cynic and the idealist. A real cross section.
SCOOP. Heidi, honey, calm down.
HEIDI. (*Quite angry.*) You have no right to call me honey, or tell me to calm down.
SCOOP. It's not my fault you didn't say anything.
HEIDI. Excuse me. I have to meet a painter downtown.
SCOOP. Who?
HEIDI. No one you know. "C" technique. "A+" use of color.
SCOOP. Andrea Rothstein.
HEIDI. How do you know Andrea Rothstein?
SCOOP. You obviously don't read *Boomer* magazine.
HEIDI. No.
SCOOP. Andrea was last week's "Hot Spot".
PETER. I once heard the same thing about Bertrand Russell.
HEIDI. Oh, please, Peter. I have to go.
SCOOP. Stay a minute. Heidella, I never see you. I'd love to talk. What's new?
HEIDI. That painter is waiting for me.
SCOOP. (*Puts his arm around her.*) Heidella, work just isn't enough. That's what I've learned.
HEIDI. Scoop, I came to talk about Women in Art.
SCOOP. You're such a wonderful person. You deserve someone wonderful. Heidi, you're clutching your purse.

53

HEIDI. I have valuables. I'm very late. (*She exits.*)

SCOOP. (*Calling after her.*) Come to the house and see us. We miss you. (*To Peter.*) I didn't mean to upset her. We were once very close.

PETER. Yup.

SCOOP. You and she are still very close.

PETER. Yup.

SCOOP. That's nice. You know, I'm sorry we never really got to know each other. You seem like a very nice man.

PETER. Are you having a sentimental spasm? You seem to be sorry, moved and touched at the drop of a hat. It's sort of manic.

SCOOP. Fatherhood changes people.

PETER. Oh, please . . .

SCOOP. Heidi says that. "Oh, please." You and Heidi have managed to maintain your friendship. I envy you that. How do you do it?

PETER. Scoop, I'd like to leave before April gets back.

SCOOP. Peter, do people like you ever wonder what it's all for?

PETER. People like you run the world. You decide what it's all for.

SCOOP. You know what genuinely surprises me? You're a far more arrogant man than I am.

PETER. Scoop, I'm just a simple man of medicine. And now I leave you to await the rebirth of wonder. (*He exits. Scoop stares out.*)

END SCENE

Scene 3

1984, Heidi is sitting at the table in a trendy N.Y. restaurant. She looks around and waits. Susan enters waving at other people in the restaurant.

SUSAN. Sorry I was on the phone so long. But we have four shows shooting. (*She waves.*) I just know everybody in this restaurant. There must be no one in L.A. Everybody's here. Honey, I'm so glad you called me. It's so nice to see you.

HEIDI. It's nice to see you too.

SUSAN. I'm famished. Are you famished? Why hasn't lunch come yet? The service here is very slow. So where were we? I want to know everything. What did you say you've been doing recently?

HEIDI. I've been working. I got a grant to put together a small show of Lilla Cabot Perry. She was an American painter from the Cabot Lowell family who spent ten years living next door to Monet.

SUSAN. Are you writing?

HEIDI. A little. "Women and Art." "Women and Madness." "Women and Bran." The usual.

SUSAN. Jesus, I miss talking to real people. Waiter, where is our lunch? We've been sitting here for at least an hour. So, Heidi, dear. Sex and violence. Are you seeing anyone?

HEIDI. Well, there's this lawyer. He calls me "darling" and says he loves me but he doesn't like me to call him after ten o'clock.

SUSAN. Oh, I hate curfews.

HEIDI. So, no, there's no one important.

SUSAN. I just broke up with my boyfriend. He's fabulous! But he's 56, and he doesn't want to start another family. And I at least want to keep my options open. I tell you Heidi, it's rough. Every other woman I know is either pregnant or just miscarried. Honestly, I've been to more fertility lunches.

HEIDI. I'm planning to start my family at sixty. I hear there's a hormone in Brazil.

SUSAN. Honey, we'll shoot a movie there and take treatments.

HEIDI. Susie, do you ever feel . . .

SUSAN. Heidi, if we've reached the part of the conversation when I tell you what I did alone for my thirty-fifth birthday, I am frankly not interested.

HEIDI. It's not that. It's just . . .

SUSAN. You know, you've developed this bizarre habit of not finishing sentences. Good thing in your business you don't have to take too many meetings.

HEIDI. Susie, do you ever think what makes you a person is also what keeps you from being a person?

SUSAN. I'm sorry, honey. But you're too deep for me. By now I've been so many people, I don't know who I am. And I

55

don't care. (*She laughs.*) Honey, I've been thinking a lot about you and how much I love you and I promise I have the answer for both of us. I'm just waiting to tell you when Denise gets here.

HEIDI. Denise!

SUSAN. Yes, Lisa's sister Denise. I hired her as my assistant. She's so quick. She's already a story editor. She's just adorable.

HEIDI. But, Susie, I called you because I was hoping we could talk . . .

SUSAN. Honey, of course we're going to talk. Nobody goes to lunch to eat. Oh, good, there's Denise. (*Denise comes over to the table, followed by the waiter.*) So what did you tell him?

DENISE. I said we respect him and his talents, and that's why we bought the property. But we have no creative slot for him. Period. (*Denise kisses Heidi.*) Hi, Heidi. It's great to see you again.

HEIDI. You too. Congratulations on your job.

DENISE. Thanks. I'm very lucky. I work for a pretty incredible lady.

SUSAN. So, you hungry?

DENISE. No, I'll just have coffee.

SUSAN. Waiter, one coffee. And I'll have my swordfish dry. No butter at all. (*Waiter leaves.*) Heidi, when I told Denise you called me yesterday we were both very excited. Besides for the obvious reason that we love you and miss you and you're one of our favorite people in the world. These bread sticks are fabulous! For a while now I've been wanting to put together a half hour show about three women turning thirty in a large urban center. It can be New York, Chicago, Houston. There are at least ten other single women series currently being developed. But your history with women and art could make us a little different.

DENISE. They've already done doctors, lawyers, nurses, and detectives. But when you called, we realized that no one has touched the art world.

SUSAN. What we're interested in is, say, a way-out painter, an uptight curator, and a dilettante heiress in a loft.

HEIDI. In Houston?

SUSAN. Wherever. You don't have to write. We'll hire a

writer. It's a package and we want you as our consultant.

HEIDI. Susie, I'm an art historian and essayist . . . I'm very flattered but . . .

SUSAN. Maybe some network executive who actually read a book five years ago will recognize your name and buy the pilot . . . (*The waiter arrives.*)

WAITER. Salmon and the Swordfish.

SUSAN. (*She looks at her plate and calls to the Waiter.*) I'm sorry. I see butter on this. I can't eat butter.

WAITER. I told them no butter.

SUSAN. Well, they didn't listen. Don't bring it back. I don't have the time. Heidi, you and I are people who need to commit. I'm not political anymore. I mean, equal rights is one thing, equal pay is one thing, but blaming everything on being a woman is just passé.

DENISE. Really.

SUSAN. Okay, three gals on the town in an apartment. Curators, painters, sculptors, what have you.

DENISE. All we need is three pages. Who these people are. Why they're funny.

HEIDI. But I have no idea who these people are. Or why they're funny.

DENISE. They're ambitious, they're professional, and they're on their way to being successful.

SUSAN. And they don't want to make the same mistakes we did.

HEIDI. I don't want to make the same mistakes we did. What exactly were they?

DENISE. Well, like, a lot of women your age are very unhappy. Unfulfilled, frightened of growing old alone.

HEIDI. It's a good thing we're not doing a sitcom about them.

DENISE. Oh, I know. I can't imagine my life without my husband or my baby Max. My friends want to get married in their twenties, have their first baby by thirty, and make a pot of money. It's just much more together than your generation.

SUSAN. (*Looking out.*) Is that Diane Keaton? I think that's Diane Keaton. Heidi, you'll come to L.A. next week. We'll meet with the network and get going on this. Diane looks terrific! I'd love to get her into a series. But until Meryl does a series, none of them will do a series.

HEIDI. Susie, I can't do it either.

DENISE. Why not?

HEIDI. Because I don't think we made such big mistakes. And I don't want to see three gals on the town who do.

DENISE. (*Denise opens her Filofax.*) Listen, if you don't like this, let's come up with something else. How about a performance artist married to a Korean grocer and living with his entire family in Queens?

SUSAN. I don't think so. Honey, all we know is sitcom is big, art is big, and women are big. Like your friend Lily Perry.

HEIDI. (*Slowly.*) Her name is Lilla and she's not my friend. Her dates are 1848 to 1933.

SUSAN. Always the historian. You know, I miss "The Heidi Chronicles." In L.A., everyone creates their own history. Honey, I would love to work with you. I think we could have a lot of fun. And that's not so terrible.

DENISE. Definitely.

SUSAN. Denise, I think Diane is leaving.

DENISE. Oh, I'll go catch her.

SUSAN. Lunch is on me.

DENISE. Heidi, I hope we didn't offend you.

SUSAN. Heidi's not offended. She just doesn't want to do it.

DENISE. (*Extends her hand.*) Goodbye, Heidi.

HEIDI. Goodbye, Denise. I'm sorry I didn't have a creative slot for you.

DENISE. (*Rushes out.*) Diane!

SUSAN. (*She kisses Heidi.*) Bye, honey. Don't forget we have a date for hormones in Brazil. Wish me luck. (*She waves as she did at the high school dance.*)

HEIDI. (*Looking after her.*) Keep the faith.

END SCENE

Scene 4

1986, The Plaza Hotel. Over loudspeaker we hear the voiceover of Sandra Zucker-Hall. "Good afternoon. I'm

Sandra Zucker-Hall, President of the Miss Crain's School East Coast Alumnae Association. The topic for today's luncheon is "Women, Where Are We Going," and we are very pleased to have as our speaker a distinguished alumna, Dr. Heidi Holland." Heidi, very well-dressed and uncomfortable, approaches a podium.

HEIDI. Hello. Hello. I graduated from Miss Crain's in 1965, and I look back on my education in Chicago very fondly. One of the far-reaching habits I developed at Miss Crain's was waiting until the desperation point to complete, or rather, start my homework. Keeping that noble academic tradition alive, I appear before you today with no formal speech. I have no outline, no pink notecards, no hieroglyphics scribbled on my palm. Nothing.

Well, you might be thinking, this is a women's meeting, so let's give her the benefit of the doubt. After teaching at Columbia yesterday, Miss Holland probably attended a low-impact aerobics class *with* weights, picked up her children from school, brought the older one to drawing with computers at the Metropolitan, and the younger one to swimming for gifted children. On returning home, she immediately prepared grilled mesquite free-range chicken with balsamic vinegar and sun-dried tomatoes, advised her investment banker/well-rounded husband on the future finances for the City Ballet, put the children to bed, recited their favorite Greek myths and sex education legends, dashed into the library to call the 22-year-old squash player who is passionately in love with her to say that they can only be friends, finished writing ten pages of a new book, brought the remains of the mesquite free-range dinner to a Church that feeds the homeless, massaged her husband's feet, and relieved any fears that he "might" be getting old by "doing it" in the kitchen, read forty pages of the *Inferno* in Italian, took a deep breath, and put out the light. So after all this, we forgive Miss Holland for not preparing a speech today. She's exemplary and exhausted.

Thank you, but you forgive too easily. And I respect my fellow alumnae enough to know that I should attempt to tell

59

you the truth. Oh, hurry up, Heidi. Okay. Why don't I have a speech for the "Women, Where Are We Going" luncheon? Well, actually, yesterday I did teach at Columbia. We discussed Alexander Pope and his theory of the picturesque. And afterwards I did attend an exercise class. I walked into the locker room, to my favorite corner, where I can pull on my basic black leotard in peace. Two ladies, younger than me, in pressed blue jeans, were heatedly debating the reading program at Marymount Nursery School, and a woman my mother's age was going on and on about her son at Harvard Law School and his wife, a Brazilian hairdresser, who was by no stretch of the imagination good enough for him. They were joined by Mrs. Green, who has perfect red nails, and confessed to anyone who would listen the hardship of throwing her dinner party on the same night as a benefit at the Met. And in the middle of them was a naked gray-haired woman extolling the virtues of brown rice and women's fiction.

And then two twenty-seven-year-old hotshots came in. How do I know they were hotshots? They were both draped in purple and green leather. And as soon as they entered the locker room they pulled out their alligator datebooks and began to madly call the office. They seemed to have everything under control. They even brought their own heavier weights.

Now Jeanette, the performance artist/dancer/actress/aerobics teacher comes in and completes the locker room. I like Jeanette. I've never talked to her, but I like her. I feel her parents are psychiatrists in the Midwest. Maybe Cedar Rapids.

Jeanette takes off her blue jeans and rolls her tights up her legs. I notice the hotshots checking out Jeanette's muscle tone while they are lacing up their Zeus low-impact sneakers, and Mrs. Green stops talking about her dinner party to ask, where did they find them? Everywhere she has looked on Madison Avenue is out. And the lady with the son at Harvard joins in and says she saw Zeus sneakers at Lord and Taylor and were they any good. Her daughter-in-law likes them, but she can't be trusted. The mothers with the pressed blue jeans leap to her rescue. Yes, they can assure her, despite the daughter-in-law, unequivocally, absolutely, no doubt about it, Zeus sneakers are the best.

It was at this point that I decided I would slip out and take my place in the back row of the class.

I picked up my overstuffed bag. But as I was just between Mrs. Green's raccoon coat and a purple leather bomber jacket, I tripped on one of the hotshots Goddamned five-pound professional weights, and out of my bag flew a week's worth of change, raspberry gum wrappers, and *Alexander Pope on the Picturesque* right on the gray-haired fiction woman's foot.

I began giggling. "Oh." "That's okay." "Excuse me." "I'm sorry." "I'm sorry I don't wear leather pants." "I'm sorry I don't eat brown rice." "I'm sorry I don't want to stand naked and discuss Zeus sneakers." "I'm sorry I don't want you to find out I'm worthless. And superior." (*Pause.*) I'm embarrassed, no humiliated in front of every woman in that room. I'm envying women I don't even know. I'm envying women I don't even like. I'm sure the woman with the son at Harvard is miserable to her daughter-in-law. I'm sure the gray-haired fiction woman is having a bisexual relationship with a female dock worker and driving her husband crazy. I'm sure the hotshots have screwed a lot of 35-year-old women, my classmates even, out of jobs, raises and husbands. And I'm sure the mothers in the pressed blue jeans think women like me chose the wrong road. "A pity they made such a mistake, that empty generation." Well, I really don't want to be feeling this way about all of them. And I certainly don't want to be feeling this way about "Women — Where are We Going?"

I hear whispers. I hear chairs moving from side to side. Yes, I see. I have one minute left.

The women start filing out of the locker room. Jeanette ties her hair in a ponytail and winks at me, "See you in class, Heidi. Don't forget to take a mat this time."

And I look at her pink and kind face. "I'm sorry, Jeanette, I think I'm too sad to go to class."

"Excuse me?" she smiles and grabs a mat.

And suddenly I stop competing with all of them. Suddenly, I'm not even racing. "To tell you the truth, Jeanette, I think I better not exercise today."

"Is there anything I can do?" she puts her arm around me. "Are you not well?"

"No, Jeanette, I'm just not happy. I'm afraid I haven't been happy for some time." (*She looks up at the audience.*)

I don't blame the ladies in the locker room for how I feel. I don't blame any of us. We're all concerned, intelligent, good women. (*Pause.*) It's just that I feel stranded. And I thought the whole point was that we wouldn't feel stranded. I thought the point was we were all in this together.

Thank you. (*She walks off.*)

END SCENE

Scene 5

1987, a children's ward in a New York Hospital. On the TV is a late night Christmas movie like "Miracle on 34th Street." A young man in a doctor's uniform is sitting on a child's chair and smoking. There are various toys and stuffed animals on the floor. There are faded Christmas decorations. Heidi awkwardly enters the room carrying boxes with records and toys, as Dr. Ray turns off the television.

HEIDI. Excuse me. Can you help me? I just have one more box.

RAY. (*Sits up.*) What?

HEIDI. I just . . .

RAY. I'm sorry, the children's ward is closed to visitors after nine o'clock. Can you come back tomorrow?

HEIDI. Well, actually, no, I can't. Well, I want to make a donation. So I'd like to, uh, drop this off tonight. Maybe if you could, tell Dr. Patrone.

RAY. I'm sorry, he's on the phone. (*Peter enters, quite agitated.*)

PETER. Heidi!

HEIDI. Peter.

PETER. (*Curt.*) What are you doing here?

HEIDI. This is a men's and women's hospital and I feel the

62

art here does not reflect the make-up of its constituency. So. So. You tell him.

RAY. She's making a donation.

PETER. At midnight!

HEIDI. I tried to reach you all week to say I was coming. Are you here every night?

PETER. When I'm not at the track.

HEIDI. Peter . . .

PETER. (*Very angry.*) Heidi, you don't burst into a Goddamn hospital at midnight because you have boyfriend trouble or some other nonsense! Sorry, Ray.

HEIDI. Sorry, Ray.

RAY. That's okay. (*He extends his hand.*) Thank you for your generous gifts. Merry Christmas.

HEIDI. Merry Christmas. (*He exits.*) He seems very nice.

PETER. You seem completely insane.

HEIDI. I have been trying to reach you.

PETER. Well, I'm here every night. It's a hectic social schedule. Cha-cha lessons at five, cocktails and limbo party at six, dinner under the stars at seven, and free love with safe sex at eight.

HEIDI. I thought you went home to Chicago. I found out you were working through the holidays in some Metropolitan News column.

PETER. It was The New York *Times.* "Science Tuesday." Page C1. What did you think of the picture?

HEIDI. I thought you looked good.

PETER. I thought I looked jowly. Turned out the photographer was an ex very close personal friend of Stanley's. He certainly made sure no one would call me. Not even you.

HEIDI. I called you. I couldn't find you.

PETER. Enough. End of narcissism. What can I do for you?

HEIDI. (*Kisses him.*) Merry Christmas.

PETER. (*Chilly.*) Thank you.

HEIDI. You're brimming with holiday cheer.

PETER. Heidi, last night three immune-deficient children in Queens were burned out of their home because an entire neighborhood preferred they not return to school next year. I don't know who the hell wants to get in here at midnight. But I can assure you that I'm not very happy that they can.

HEIDI. I should have called again.

PETER. I'm sorry, Heidi. I'm not feeling very communicative. Unfortunately, things here are for real. Not farina.

HEIDI. I've never heard that. For real. Not farina.

PETER. Stanley used it.

HEIDI. How is Stanley?

PETER. Oh, he's fine. What's all this?

HEIDI. Nothing.

PETER. This gets better and better. You came here at midnight, Christmas Eve with boxes of nothing.

HEIDI. It's boxes of books. Records. Clothing. One girl's complete collection.

PETER. Thank you. We accept. Winter cleaning before the New Year?

HEIDI. (*Mumbling.*) No, well, actually, I'm leaving tomorrow.

PETER. Heidi, you're mumbling.

HEIDI. I'm going away tomorrow.

PETER. Chicago. See your parents.

HEIDI. I'm going to Northfield, Minnesota. Where the Jesse James band was stopped.

PETER. Are you planning to rob banks and get caught?

HEIDI. I thought I'd finish my new book in the Midwest. I had an offer to teach at Carleton College there. So I accepted.

PETER. (*Surprised.*) This is sudden.

HEIDI. Well, yes, but . . .

PETER. But why not?

HEIDI. Peter. I came to say goodbye.

PETER. Goodbye.

HEIDI. That's it?

PETER. What do you want me to say?

HEIDI. I don't know. You'll call me.

PETER. I'll call you. Heidi, what do you want me to say? You're a brave and remarkable woman. A proud pioneer. My Antonia driving ever forward through the unknown.

HEIDI. (*Softly.*) Peter, sweetie, what is it?

PETER. (*Moves away.*) Nothing. (*He begins straightening the room, putting toys away.*) So you're going to Northfield, Minnesota to start again. Goodbye, New York. Goodbye, mistakes. Make new friends. Give donations to the old.

64

HEIDI. I hate it when you're like this.

PETER. Heidi, you arrived at midnight and promptly announced you're leaving tomorrow. I'm just feeling my way through this.

HEIDI. I thought you would be the person who would completely understand.

PETER. (*Quite angry.*) Understand what? Looking back at your life and regretting your choices? Deciding your work, your friends, your history are totally expendable.

HEIDI. You have a life here that works for you. I don't.

PETER. Right. So I am expendable, too.

HEIDI. Peter, stop it!

PETER. (*Very distant.*) I'm not doing anything. I was going to spend a quiet Christmas here with the Hardy Boys.

HEIDI. The Hardy Boys?

PETER. For our last midnight donation, we received my sister-in-law Paula Patrone's complete childhood collection of Nancy Drew, the Bobbsey Twins, the Hardy Boys, Honey Bunch, and *Heidi,* which I actually perused last night in your honor. (*He picks up a book from the floor.*) Did you know that the first section is Heidi's year of travel and learning, and the second is Heidi uses what she knows? (*Softly.*) How will you use what you know, Heidi?

HEIDI. I've been sad for a long time. I don't want to be sad anymore.

PETER. This is hard, Heidi. This is very hard. (*He begins going through her boxes.*) What have we got here? The Mamas and the Papas, Gerry and the Pacemakers, Sam the Sham and the Pharoahs. (*He picks up a record.*) "Theodore Bikel Sings Favorite Worksongs from the Fourth International."

HEIDI. Scoop's. From his red diaper period.

PETER. H.W. Jansen, *A History of Art*; Jakob Rosenberg, *Rembrandt's Life and Work*; *The Secret Life of Salvador Dali*; Alice Elizabeth Chase, *Famous Paintings — An Introduction for Young People*; *Mary Cassatt and Philadelphia.* Thank you. We don't have any of these.

HEIDI. (*Smiles.*) I thought not.

PETER. The next time some reporter arrives with a surly photographer, I'll tell them, "Never mind the kids' immune system, ask them about the secret life of Salvador Dali."

HEIDI. I think your starting this unit is remarkable.

65

PETER. Your friend Susan's production company sent us a very nice check. Who would have thought three women in a Houston loft would capture the national imagination? It's odd what people find comforting.

HEIDI. What, sweetie?

PETER. Nothing. I was thinking about what people find comforting. I'm sorry. Generally, I try to stay fairly chipper.

HEIDI. Honey, you don't have to be chipper around me.

PETER. You know what's as unappealing in its own insidious way as my sarcasm?

HEIDI. What?

PETER. Your trying too hard. The high voice, the gratuitous "honey" or "sweetie." I can't tell what the hell you're thinking! (*He throws one of the dolls across the room.*)

HEIDI. Peter, where is all this coming from?

PETER. Truth.

HEIDI. It'd be preferable.

PETER. Okay. Heidi, I'd say about once a month now I gather in some church, meeting house or concert hall with handsome men all my own age, and in the front row is usually a couple my parents' age, the father's in a suit and the mother's tasteful, a pleasant face. And we listen for half an hour to testimonials, memories, amusing anecdotes about a son, a friend, a lover, also handsome, also usually my own age, whom none of us will see again. After the first, the fifth, or the fifteenth of these gatherings, a sadness like yours seems a luxury.

HEIDI. I understand.

PETER. No, you don't. Not really. I left out one other thing. My friend Stanley isn't very well. That was my call when you so adventurously arrived. That's where all this is coming from.

HEIDI. Peter, I . . .

PETER. (*Quietly, with feeling.*) You see, my world gets narrower and narrower. A person only has so many close friends. And in our lives, our friends are our families. I'm actually quite hurt you don't understand that. I'm very sorry you don't find that comforting.

HEIDI. There is no one precious to me in the way you are.

PETER. But obviously I can't help you. And you can't help

me. So . . .

HEIDI. So . . .

PETER. My best to Jesse James. (*Pause.*)

HEIDI. Peter, we could try.

PETER. Not if you're off to become someone else.

HEIDI. I could become someone else next year. Postpone it. If that's not a little too understanding.

PETER. A little, but I'm listening.

HEIDI. I promise you won't lose this member of your family.

PETER. Who? The sad one or the one I spotted twenty-five years ago at a Miss Crain's School dance?

HEIDI. Split the difference? (*Pause.*)

PETER. However, if you do stay, I have one specific request.

HEIDI. What?

PETER. That you still plan to donate this very fine collection.

HEIDI. All yours. (*Peter begins going through the records again.*)

PETER. Mitch Ryder and the Detroit Wheels. Gary Puckett and the Union Gap. Nelson and the Rocky Fellers. How did we ever become friends?

HEIDI. I'm a sucker for a man of taste and talent.

PETER. You have such distinguished taste in music. I can tell you're very bright. Tell me, since I value your fine opinion, what did you think of Dr. Ray? (*He sits in one of the children's chairs.*)

HEIDI. I told you I liked him. (*Heidi sits in a child's chair beside him.*)

PETER. Yes. And I like Greg Louganis. But I don't know if a diver is the best choice for me.

HEIDI. Is Dr. Ray a diver?

PETER. No. But he's a man of taste and talent.

HEIDI. (*Picks up two dixie cups.*) It's a lovely evening, don't you think?

PETER. What?

HEIDI. The stars above us. The sea below us. Tell me, how long have you been on this cruise?

PETER. Oh, around twenty-five years. I tried to pick out your name. Amanda, Lady Clara, Estelle.

HEIDI. (*She notices him crying.*) It's . . .

PETER. I know. It's Heidi. Your old grandfather told me. Are you from the Alps?
HEIDI. Yes. Like chocolate. I want to know you all my life. If we can't marry, let's be great friends.
PETER. I will keep this goblet as a memento beside my pillow. (*He looks at her. She takes his hand and gets him up.*)
HEIDI. Ah, "The Shoop Shoop Song." Baroque but fragile.
PETER. I'm not familiar with the work. (*She begins to sing very softly to him.*)
HEIDI. "Is it in her eyes?"
PETER. (*Very softly, after a moment.*) "Oh, no, you'll be deceived."
HEIDI. "If you want to know if she loves you so . . ." (*Peter embraces Heidi.*)*
PETER. Merry Christmas, Heidi.
HEIDI. Merry Christmas, Peter.

END SCENE

SCENE 6

1989, an empty room with fireplace. The room has been freshly painted white. Warm afternoon sunlight streams through the window. A rocker. Heidi, seated, is reading through a book galley. Scoop enters. He is dressed for a business lunch in a suit and raincoat.

SCOOP. (*Loud.*) Hello. Hello.
HEIDI. Scoop!
SCOOP. Hello. I'm canvassing for Eugene McCarthy for president. Miss Holland, you might be interested in my publication. *The Liberated Earth News.* We tell the truth. The way the people see it. So what's up? This is a nice apartment. What do they call it? Raw space with rocker?
HEIDI. I moved in last week. Furniture hasn't come yet.
SCOOP. You know what you could use here? Chintz. Chintz curtains would be very nice. But not shiny. Be specific.
HEIDI. What do you know about chintz?
SCOOP. Now that's sexist. That's really sexist. I've deco-

---

*Used by permission. See note on page 81.

rated at least four houses, and I've edited a magazine for ten years that was responsible for the chintz renaissance as we know it today. In fact, do you know why warm Mediterranean colors have returned to the home palette?

HEIDI. Because *Boomer* magazine warned us against the disastrous side effects of too many pastels. Scoop, what are you doing here?

SCOOP. Maritime art.

HEIDI. You came to my raw space for maritime art?

SCOOP. I have an offer to buy maritime art. April Lambert's husband is into equestrian art. So horses are out of the question for me. But I'm considering maritime art. I've always liked Turner.

HEIDI. Well, you can't go wrong with a Turner.

SCOOP. Or a Winslow Homer. So, are you happy?

HEIDI. What?

SCOOP. I made a list the other day of the people I care about. And you made the top ten. In fact, I reworked the list a few times, and you were the only one who made the top ten through three decades. Yup. You and Smokey Robinson were the standards. So if I can keep you on my list, you can tell me if you're happy and why. Mmmm. Good cookies.

HEIDI. "A+" pecan. "B—" sandy.

SCOOP. Better. "B+" sandy.

HEIDI. Actually, I am seeing an editor I seem to like.

SCOOP. Good. Time for my life now. See, I've grown over the years. We did you first. I think that shows remarkable control and sensitivity. Can you keep a secret?

HEIDI. If this involves someone in fishnets twenty-five or younger, not really.

SCOOP. I hate it when you're prissy. Does your editor know you're prissy?

HEIDI. Yes. He's even more prissy than I am. Scoop, why are you here?

SCOOP. Touch base. There aren't that many people in my life who really know me. I sold *Boomer* magazine two hours ago. You're the first to know.

HEIDI. What? Why?

SCOOP. I was at lunch at Lutece with the potential buyer and his lawyer and I made a deal with myself. If I could get the lemon souffle without ordering a day in advance, I'd sell. Have you ever ordered souffle in advance at Lutece?

HEIDI. No.

SCOOP. Do it.

HEIDI. I don't want to.

SCOOP. Pick up the phone and do it! This is the best dessert I've ever had.

HEIDI. Scoop, stop it.

SCOOP. (*He dials.*) Hi, it's Scoop Rosenbaum. I'd like to order two souffles for tonight.

HEIDI. Scoop, I'm not going to Lutece for dinner tonight. And I'm certainly not dropping in for dessert. I'm busy.

SCOOP. We're undecided, lemon or chocolate. I'll call back. Thank you. (*He hangs up.*)

HEIDI. I have a date.

SCOOP. With who? That editorial drone? Where did he go to school? You're not missing a lemon souffle at Lutece for an intimate evening dangling participles. (*He dials the phone again.*) Hello. This is Mr. Rosenbaum. Who is this? Ah, bonjour, Phillipe. Comment allez-vous?

HEIDI. Scoop, where's Lisa?

SCOOP. She's in Florida with Maggie and her mother. Pierre's in town with me.

HEIDI. Maybe we should call Lisa.

SCOOP. No, we shouldn't call Lisa. (*On the phone.*) Phillipe. Deux citron souffles.

HEIDI. All right. Maybe we should call someone else?

SCOOP. You mean, is there a fishnet somewhere in town so you don't have to deal with me tonight?

HEIDI. Something like that. Yes.

SCOOP. No such luck. Phillipe, je je . . . (*He hangs up.*) Merci. (*Scoop begins to sing.*) "Baby, I'm yours. And I'll be yours until two and two are three."*

HEIDI. Did you really sell your magazine?

SCOOP. Yup.

HEIDI. Why?

SCOOP. Because I wanted to buy maritime art. Do you know how much they paid me?

---

*Used by permission. See note on page 81.

HEIDI. No.

SCOOP. I think this raw space could do with a Turner or two. I'll get you a few for Christmas.

HEIDI. But why did you do it?

SCOOP. What's it all for, Heidella? What's it all for?

HEIDI. You liked it.

SCOOP. Yup.

HEIDI. You were good at it.

SCOOP. Yup. And I stopped pastels in the nick of time. And I helped get a few people elected, and a few people investigated, and a single man who likes oral sex when he reads the Talmud placed an ad and married a woman who doesn't. I did all that. Now what?

HEIDI. What do you mean?

SCOOP. Now what? What do I show my children and say "See, kids, Daddy did that"? Do I say, "See that restaurant, Maggie? Daddy started going there and suddenly everybody was going there until they started going somewhere else"? Do I say, "Pierre, your father was known as an arbiter of good taste in a decade defined as sexy, greedy"? Or is my greatest legacy to them buying a farm in Litchfield County before the land value went soaring. Will my kids say, "My dad was basically a lazy man and a philanderer, but he had a nose for Connecticut real estate and we love him because he didn't make us weekend in the Hamptons."

HEIDI. I didn't know you worried so much about your children.

SCOOP. I'm sorry. I mean, we hardly know each other anymore. I'm sorry. (*He looks at her.*) I'm being very self-indulgent. Yes?

HEIDI. Yes.

SCOOP. I'm a spoiled man with superficial values. Yes?

HEIDI. Don't look at me like that.

SCOOP. Like what?

HEIDI. Don't look at me with those doe eyes and tell me how spoiled you are. Next thing I know you'll tell me you never meant to hurt me.

SCOOP. Maybe we should try again.

HEIDI. Why?

SCOOP. You're lonely and I'm lost.

71

HEIDI. Oh, please. (*Pause. They both laugh.*)

SCOOP. (*Smiles.*) I thought you might enjoy that.

HEIDI. I did. A lot.

SCOOP. How much?

HEIDI. (*Smiles.*) A lot.

SCOOP. So as my old friend and long time observer, what do you think I should do now?

HEIDI. I'd say hold on to the land in Litchfield County. (*Scoop kisses Heidi on the cheek.*)

SCOOP. It's nice to see you, Heidella.

HEIDI. It's nice to see you. I have absolutely no idea why Lisa stays married to you.

SCOOP. You would have married me.

HEIDI. But I wouldn't have stayed married to you.

SCOOP. Good thing I'm married to Lisa.

HEIDI. Yup. Good thing.

SCOOP. I never liked your caustic side. You and Peter share that. How is Peter?

HEIDI. Peter moved in with a nice anesthesiologist named Ray. He still runs that ward and on weekends they garden at their home in Bucks County.

SCOOP. A handsome doctor and a country house. Peter's living my mother's dream come true! I thought of you both last week when I was flying home from L.A.

HEIDI. You did?

SCOOP. It was nighttime and I recognized Chicago from the sky and I remembered the first time I visited you there. Remember, I spent the day asking for Goethe Street, until I called and you said "Dummy, it's pronounced "Go-the." Anyway, I wondered if flying over Chicago for my grand-children would be like driving past an A&W root beer stand for me. I think about the future all the time now.

HEIDI. Scoop, you didn't sell *Boomer* for a lemon souffle.

SCOOP. Heidi, on a scale from one to ten, if you aim for six and get six, that's the ballgame. So you might as well try for your ten.

HEIDI. If you know what your ten is.

SCOOP. Well, I have a notion. Oh, yes, and one other thing. Susan told me you adopted a baby last week.

72

HEIDI. She did?

SCOOP. Yes. And I thought, "Fuck you. If you have the courage to make the move and go for your ten, then what am I waiting for?"

HEIDI. Wait a minute! Why is my baby my ten, and your work is your ten?

SCOOP. I didn't mean it that way.

HEIDI. Well, it certainly came out that way. I'm not some empty vessel.

SCOOP. (Smiling.) No, you're not. But I appreciate the maritime allusion.

HEIDI. And anyway, I wasn't alone against the wilderness. Peter helped me. Shall I get off my high horse now, or would you like to hear more?

SCOOP. You're cute.

HEIDI. You're deceptive. She's asleep in the other raw space.

SCOOP. This entire time? Why didn't you say anything?

HEIDI. Why didn't you say anything?

SCOOP. What do you call her?

HEIDI. Vicious dumpling.

SCOOP. Really!

HEIDI. Peter suggested Panama Hattie in honor of his favorite musical and her place of birth.

SCOOP. Certainly a noticeable college application.

HEIDI. I also considered Lilla, Mary, or Grandma, so she'll grow up to be a painter. And Crystal or Ronnette so she'll grow up to start a girl group. But that's a little . . .

SCOOP. Much. That's a little much.

HEIDI. So I settled on Judy. After "A Date with Judy." She's very pretty. A little cellulite on the toes, but by the time she's 20, they'll be doing simple nips and toe tucks at Elizabeth Arden.

SCOOP. And are you happy?

HEIDI. I've never been what I'd call a happy girl. Too prissy. Too caustic.

SCOOP. But now. Right now. Are you happy?

HEIDI. Well, I have a daughter. And I've never been particularly maternal. I'm not real practiced at sharing. But,

73

Scoop, there's a chance. Just a milli-notion. That Pierre Rosenbaum and Judy Holland will meet on a plane over Chicago. And Pierre will tell her his father named him for a Canadian Prime Minister, and she'll say she was almost named for someone who sang "My Boyfriend's Back." And he'll never tell her it's either/or baby. And she'll never think she's worthless unless he lets her have it all. And maybe, just maybe, things will be a little better. And yes, that does make me happy.

SCOOP. So I was right all along. You were a true believer.

HEIDI. I don't see how it could be any other way.

SCOOP. No regrets.

HEIDI. Just two.

SCOOP. Me?

HEIDI. No. "Hello New York" and I still never torched lingerie.

SCOOP. (*Suddenly looking at his watch.*) Jesus, *The Wicked Cooks!*

HEIDI. Who?

SCOOP. *The Wicked Cooks,* it's a Gunther Grass novel. Pierre's music teacher adapted it for the fourth grade play at Ethical Culture.

HEIDI. Why don't they do "The Music Man" or "Johnny Appleseed"?

SCOOP. Oh, please. (*He pulls out a package from his pocket.*) This is for Judy. It's a silver spoon. My secretary picked it out. You can't go wrong.

HEIDI. Hey, Scoop, I think you did the right thing.

SCOOP. Buying the spoon or selling the magazine?

HEIDI. Both. Don't you want to just take a peek at Judy? Stay just a sec. I want her to understand men, and you're a classic. (*She leaves the room.*)

SCOOP. (*Calls to her.*) I'm sort of dating an actress who says I'm withholding. Do you think I'm withholding?

HEIDI. Well, let's just say I don't know who you're saving it for. (*Heidi returns with carriage.*) Judy Holland, this is Scoop Rosenbaum.

SCOOP. Hi, Judy.

HEIDI. Hi, Scoop.

74

SCOOP. How ya doing? They all look like Winston Churchill. "A+" intelligence, "B—" vocabulary.

HEIDI. C'mon, be generous. "A+" vocabulary.

SCOOP. (*Looks at his watch.*) Fuck! The fucking wicked cooks!

HEIDI. Judy, for future reference, Uncle Scoop hates foul language. (*She walks him to the entry way.*) 'Bye, Scoop. Thanks for coming to see us.

SCOOP. Hey, Heidella. If I do something crazy like announce I'm running for Congress next week, will you and Peter be there? Gay men and single mothers for Rosenbaum. Grass roots movements. A man for all genders.

HEIDI. So that's why you sold your magazine.

SCOOP. All people deserve to fulfill their potential. Judy, that's what your mother told me in 1968 on the first snowy night in Manchester, New Hampshire. America needs heroes.

HEIDI. Scoop, you are many things, but . . . (*Scoop takes Heidi's hand.*)

SCOOP. What do you think, Judy? A mother for the nineties and a hero for the nineties. 'Bye, Heidella. (*He kisses her on the cheek. He exits.*)

HEIDI. (*Calls after him.*) The editor went to Columbia.

SCOOP. (*Calls back.*) I knew that! (*Heidi takes Judy out of the stroller and lifts her up.*)

HEIDI. A heroine for the twenty-first! (*She sits in the rocker and begins to sing softly, adding her own spirited high and low harmonies.*)

HEIDI. "Darling, you send me.
You send me.
Honest you do, honest you do, honest you do."*
(*Lights fade as Heidi rocks.*)

END PLAY

---

*Used by permission. See note on page 81.

SCENERY	FURNITURE	HAND PROPS
ACT I – Prologue	LECTURE HALL	
Projection Screen	Podium	Flashlight pointer
ACT I – Scene 1	MISS CRAIN'S DANCE	
Trick Wall/Bball hoop	2 folding chairs	Punch bowl w/punch, ladle
Yellow/Pink Streamers	Table w/pink tablecloth	3 stacks pink/yellow cups
		Purse w/Death Be Not Proud (c)
		Hankie (P) (pp)
		White purse w/2 necklaces, earrings (c)
ACT I – Scene 2	McCARTHY MIXER	
Trick Wall:	2 folding chairs (l-1)	Purse & name tag – Heidi Holland (c)
3 McCarthy posters	Table w/blue tablecloth	Metal bowl of chips/2 beer bottles
Poster w/sign-up sheets	Garbage can w/balloons & ice	5 beer bottles, Pepsi bottles
Fire extinguisher		Can opener on string
Red/White/Blue streamers		Tobacco & rolling papers (Drew) (pp)
		Leather bag (S) (c)
ACT I – Scene 3	RAP GROUP	
Basement curtain	2 stacks of chairs (16)	Record player & record
Hanging light fixture	A-V cart	TV tray w/coffee pot, 5 cups, saran wrap on plate of cookies (peanut butter granola)
	Metal church sign & letters	Spray bottle/water – wet coats & shoes
	2 flagpoles	Purse (H) (S) – knapsack (B) (c)

(c) = costume prop   (pp) = personal prop

ACT I - Scene 4	ART INSTITUTE OF CHICAGO	
AIC Drop	Park bench	Bullhorn
		4 umbrellas – 2 black, 1 grey, 1 green
		Backpack (P)
		Placard w/plastic cover
		Hankies (H) (P) (pp)
		Clipboard w/petition & pen
		Box of buttons – Women in Art
		AIC shopping bag w/posters
ACT I - Scene 5	PIERRE WEDDING	
Pierre Wall	2 straight back chairs	Flowers in white vase
Pierre Masking Wall	Marble topped table	2 bottles of champagne-open
	2 end tables	Silver tray for glasses
	Settee	6 champagne glasses
	3 rugs	Plate of hors d'oeuvres
	2 arm chairs	caviar, bread,
	Settee	crackers
	Standing ashtray	Peach cocktail napkins
		2 glass ashtrays
		Cigar & matches
		Hankie (S) (pp)
		Glass plate w/crackers
ACT II - Prologue	LECTURE HALL	
Projection Screen	Podium	Flashlight pointer
ACT II - Scene 1	POWER SHOWER	
Periaktoi-bookshelves	Coffee table-plexi top/metal base	Wine & Perrier bottles
	Sofa w/6 pillows & 3 cushions	5 wine glasses
	Library ladder	Baby record book & pencil
	Round end table	John Lennon albums
	Arm chair w/blue blanket	Turntable w/album
	Red wooden chair	Open Present: robe, gown & slippers
(c) = costume prop	(pp) = personal prop	

77

		Wrapped Presents:
		  leopard snuggly-gift
		  card on present
		  heffalump/FAO
		  Schwartz bag

		Hat form
		Wrapping paper
		Ribbons, bows &
		  Scotch tape
		4 open present boxes
		  & tissue paper
		Piece of gum (B) (pp)

ACT II – Scene 2
Periaktoi-Hello NY
	HELLO NEW YORK
	4 blue chairs
	Triangular coffee
	  table
	3 silver canisters
	2 plants
	2 stands w/lights
	Tall gray stool
	Flowers in glass bowl
	  on table
		Clipboard-
		  paper & pencil (S)
		Headset w/belt pack
		  (S)
		Clipboard
		  paper, index cards,
		  pen (D) (c)
		4 lavolier mics
		Index card (A) (c)
		Purse w/datebook
		  (H) (c)
		2 pieces of gum (S)
		b/w checked coffee
		  mug (A)

ACT II – Scene 3
Periaktoi-Restaurant
	RESTAURANT
	3 black/chrome
	  chairs
	Round table
	  w/white
	  tablecloth
		Tray w/2 martinis
		1 menu
		Salt & pepper
		  shakers
		2 napkin, knife,
		  spoon, 4 forks
		Bowl of flowers
		Basket of
		  breadsticks
		Perrier in glass of

(c) = costume prop   (pp) = personal prop

78

ice w/lemon
    wedge & swizzle
Tray w/cup of
    coffee on saucer
    & creamer
Waiters order pad
    & pencil
Plate of salmon,
    carrots, potatoes
Plate of swordfish,
    carrots, potatoes
Filofax & pen (D)

ACT II – Scene 4	PLAZA HOTEL	
Austrian drop	Podium	
	w/microphone	

ACT II – Scene 5   *PEDIATRICS WARD*

Pediatrics Wall   Child's table   Slider w/Xmas
Merry Christmas on   2 children's chairs   tree, TV-ON,
   Wall   Wheelchair   cart, VCR,
Strand of Xmas lights   3 wrapped boxes,
Apt. Beam   "Heidi", VCR
                                      tapes, 2 boxes
                                      wrapped presents
                                 Box of clothes
                                 2 boxes – books &
                                      records
                                 Stack of Dixie cups
                                 Lit cigarette &
                                      dixie cup (R)
                                 Firetruck w/toys:
                                      red doll, hand
                                      puppet, Raggedy
                                      Ann, clown,
                                      bunny rabbit,
                                      frog w/jacket &
                                      pants, elephant,
                                      clown, 3 Nancy
                                      Drew books,
                                      magnetic game,

(c) = costume prop   (pp) = personal prop

		slipper, rag doll, baby doll, dog, blue ostrich
ACT II – Scene 6	*HEIDI'S APARTMENT*	
French Doors	Rocking chair	Telephone w/long cord
Apt. Beam	Carriage w/baby &	Plate-pecan sandy cookies
DOOR SLAM UNIT	pink blanket	Galley & pencil (H)
		Box w/silver spoon (S)
		(tarp, paint can, paint tray)
		(6 wrapped paintings)

(c) = costume prop   (pp) = personal prop

MUSIC CREDITS

The following song excerpts have been cleared for use by groups producing "The Heidi Chronicles." No further permission is required.

The Shoop Shoop Song (It's In His Kiss)

"THE SHOOP SHOOP SONG (IT'S IN HIS KISS)" by Rudy Clark
©1963, 1964-ALLEY MUSIC CORP. and TRIO MUSIC CO., INC.
Used by permission. All rights reserved.

Respect

"RESPECT" Lyrics and music by Otis Redding.
© 1982-Irving Music, Inc. (BMI)
All Rights Reserved—International Copyright Secured.

You Send Me

"YOU SEND ME" Written by Sam Cooke
© 1957 Renewed 1985 ABKCO Music, Inc.
All Rights Reserved. Used by permission.

Baby, I'm Yours

"BABY, I'M YOURS" Written by Van McCoy.
© 1964, 1965 All Rights Administered by EMI Blackwood Music Inc.
All Rights Reserved. International Copyright Secured.
Used by Permission. Note: No permissions have been granted for performance of this song in New York City.

NEW PLAYS

★ **YELLOW FACE by David Henry Hwang.** Asian-American playwright DHH leads a protest against the casting of Jonathan Pryce as the Eurasian pimp in the original Broadway production of *Miss Saigon*, condemning the practice as "yellowface." The lines between truth and fiction blur with hilarious and moving results in this unreliable memoir. "A pungent play of ideas with a big heart." —*Variety*. "Fabulously inventive." —*The New Yorker.* [5M, 2W] ISBN: 978-0-8222-2301-6

★ **33 VARIATIONS by Moisés Kaufmann.** A mother coming to terms with her daughter. A composer coming to terms with his genius. And, even though they're separated by 200 years, these two people share an obsession that might, even just for a moment, make time stand still. "A compellingly original and thoroughly watchable play for today." —*Talkin' Broadway.* [4M, 4W] ISBN: 978-0-8222-2392-4

★ **BOOM by Peter Sinn Nachtrieb.** A grad student's online personal ad lures a mysterious journalism student to his subterranean research lab. But when a major catastrophic event strikes the planet, their date takes on evolutionary significance and the fate of humanity hangs in the balance. "Darkly funny dialogue." —*NY Times.* "Literate, coarse, thoughtful, sweet, scabrously inappropriate." —*Washington City Paper.* [1M, 2W] ISBN: 978-0-8222-2370-2

★ **LOVE, LOSS AND WHAT I WORE by Nora Ephron and Delia Ephron, based on the book by Ilene Beckerman.** A play of monologues and ensemble pieces about women, clothes and memory covering all the important subjects—mothers, prom dresses, mothers, buying bras, mothers, hating purses and why we only wear black. "Funny, compelling." —*NY Times.* "So funny and so powerful." —*WowOwow.com.* [5W] ISBN: 978-0-8222-2355-9

★ **CIRCLE MIRROR TRANSFORMATION by Annie Baker.** When four lost New Englanders enrolled in Marty's community center drama class experiment with harmless games, hearts are quietly torn apart, and tiny wars of epic proportions are waged and won. "Absorbing, unblinking and sharply funny." —*NY Times.* [2M, 3W] ISBN: 978-0-8222-2445-7

★ **BROKE-OLOGY by Nathan Louis Jackson.** The King family has weathered the hardships of life and survived with their love for each other intact. But when two brothers are called home to take care of their father, they find themselves strangely at odds. "Engaging dialogue." —*TheaterMania.com.* "Assured, bighearted." —*Time Out.* [3M, 1W] ISBN: 978-0-8222-2428-0

DRAMATISTS PLAY SERVICE, INC.
440 Park Avenue South, New York, NY 10016 212-683-8960 Fax 212-213-1539
postmaster@dramatists.com www.dramatists.com

NEW PLAYS

★ **A CIVIL WAR CHRISTMAS: AN AMERICAN MUSICAL CELEBRATION by Paula Vogel, music by Daryl Waters.** It's 1864, and Washington, D.C. is settling down to the coldest Christmas Eve in years. Intertwining many lives, this musical shows us that the gladness of one's heart is the best gift of all. "Boldly inventive theater, warm and affecting." *–Talkin' Broadway.* "Crisp strokes of dialogue." *–NY Times.* [12M, 5W] ISBN: 978-0-8222-2361-0

★ **SPEECH & DEBATE by Stephen Karam.** Three teenage misfits in Salem, Oregon discover they are linked by a sex scandal that's rocked their town. "Savvy comedy." *–Variety.* "Hilarious, cliché-free, and immensely entertaining." *–NY Times.* "A strong, rangy play." *–NY Newsday.* [2M, 2W] ISBN: 978-0-8222-2286-6

★ **DIVIDING THE ESTATE by Horton Foote.** Matriarch Stella Gordon is determined not to divide her 100-year-old Texas estate, despite her family's declining wealth and the looming financial crisis. But her three children have another plan. "Goes for laughs and succeeds." *–NY Daily News.* "The theatrical equivalent of a page-turner." *–Bloomberg.com.* [4M, 9W] ISBN: 978-0-8222-2398-6

★ **WHY TORTURE IS WRONG, AND THE PEOPLE WHO LOVE THEM by Christopher Durang.** Christopher Durang turns political humor upside down with this raucous and provocative satire about America's growing homeland "insecurity." "A smashing new play." *–NY Observer.* "You may laugh yourself silly." *–Bloomberg News.* [4M, 3W] ISBN: 978-0-8222-2401-3

★ **FIFTY WORDS by Michael Weller.** While their nine-year-old son is away for the night on his first sleepover, Adam and Jan have an evening alone together, beginning a suspenseful nightlong roller-coaster ride of revelation, rancor, passion and humor. "Mr. Weller is a bold and productive dramatist." *–NY Times.* [1M, 1W] ISBN: 978-0-8222-2348-1

★ **BECKY'S NEW CAR by Steven Dietz.** Becky Foster is caught in middle age, middle management and in a middling marriage—with no prospects for change on the horizon. Then one night a socially inept and grief-struck millionaire stumbles into the car dealership where Becky works. "Gently and consistently funny." *–Variety.* "Perfect blend of hilarious comedy and substantial weight." *–Broadway Hour.* [4M, 3W] ISBN: 978-0-8222-2393-1

DRAMATISTS PLAY SERVICE, INC.
440 Park Avenue South, New York, NY 10016 212-683-8960 Fax 212-213-1539
postmaster@dramatists.com   www.dramatists.com

NEW PLAYS

★ **AT HOME AT THE ZOO by Edward Albee.** Edward Albee delves deeper into his play THE ZOO STORY by adding a first act, HOMELIFE, which precedes Peter's fateful meeting with Jerry on a park bench in Central Park. "An essential and heartening experience." –*NY Times.* "Darkly comic and thrilling." –*Time Out.* "Genuinely fascinating." –*Journal News.* [2M, 1W] ISBN: 978-0-8222-2317-7

★ **PASSING STRANGE book and lyrics by Stew, music by Stew and Heidi Rodewald, created in collaboration with Annie Dorsen.** A daring musical about a young bohemian that takes you from black middle-class America to Amsterdam, Berlin and beyond on a journey towards personal and artistic authenticity. "Fresh, exuberant, bracingly inventive, bitingly funny, and full of heart." –*NY Times.* "The freshest musical in town!" –*Wall Street Journal.* "Excellent songs and a vulnerable heart." –*Variety.* [4M, 3W] ISBN: 978-0-8222-2400-6

★ **REASONS TO BE PRETTY by Neil LaBute.** Greg really, truly adores his girlfriend, Steph. Unfortunately, he also thinks she has a few physical imperfections, and when he mentions them, all hell breaks loose. "Tight, tense and emotionally true." –*Time Magazine.* "Lively and compulsively watchable." –*The Record.* [2M, 2W] ISBN: 978-0-8222-2394-8

★ **OPUS by Michael Hollinger.** With only a few days to rehearse a grueling Beethoven masterpiece, a world-class string quartet struggles to prepare their highest-profile performance ever—a televised ceremony at the White House. "Intimate, intense and profoundly moving." –*Time Out.* "Worthy of scores of bravissimos." –*BroadwayWorld.com.* [4M, 1W] ISBN: 978-0-8222-2363-4

★ **BECKY SHAW by Gina Gionfriddo.** When an evening calculated to bring happiness takes a dark turn, crisis and comedy ensue in this wickedly funny play that asks what we owe the people we love and the strangers who land on our doorstep. "As engrossing as it is ferociously funny." –*NY Times.* "Gionfriddo is some kind of genius." –*Variety.* [2M, 3W] ISBN: 978-0-8222-2402-0

★ **KICKING A DEAD HORSE by Sam Shepard.** Hobart Struther's horse has just dropped dead. In an eighty-minute monologue, he discusses what path brought him here in the first place, the fate of his marriage, his career, politics and eventually the nature of the universe. "Deeply instinctual and intuitive." –*NY Times.* "The brilliance is in the infinite reverberations Shepard extracts from his simple metaphor." –*TheaterMania.* [1M, 1W] ISBN: 978-0-8222-2336-8

DRAMATISTS PLAY SERVICE, INC.
440 Park Avenue South, New York, NY 10016 212-683-8960 Fax 212-213-1539
postmaster@dramatists.com www.dramatists.com

NEW PLAYS

★ **AUGUST: OSAGE COUNTY by Tracy Letts.** WINNER OF THE 2008 PULITZER PRIZE AND TONY AWARD. When the large Weston family reunites after Dad disappears, their Oklahoma homestead explodes in a maelstrom of repressed truths and unsettling secrets. "Fiercely funny and bitingly sad." *–NY Times.* "Ferociously entertaining." *–Variety.* "A hugely ambitious, highly combustible saga." *–NY Daily News.* [6M, 7W] ISBN: 978-0-8222-2300-9

★ **RUINED by Lynn Nottage.** WINNER OF THE 2009 PULITZER PRIZE. Set in a small mining town in Democratic Republic of Congo, RUINED is a haunting, probing work about the resilience of the human spirit during times of war. "A full-immersion drama of shocking complexity and moral ambiguity." *–Variety.* "Sincere, passionate, courageous." *–Chicago Tribune.* [8M, 4W] ISBN: 978-0-8222-2390-0

★ **GOD OF CARNAGE by Yasmina Reza, translated by Christopher Hampton.** WINNER OF THE 2009 TONY AWARD. A playground altercation between boys brings together their Brooklyn parents, leaving the couples in tatters as the rum flows and tensions explode. "Satisfyingly primitive entertainment." *–NY Times.* "Elegant, acerbic, entertainingly fueled on pure bile." *–Variety.* [2M, 2W] ISBN: 978-0-8222-2399-3

★ **THE SEAFARER by Conor McPherson.** Sharky has returned to Dublin to look after his irascible, aging brother. Old drinking buddies Ivan and Nicky are holed up at the house too, hoping to play some cards. But with the arrival of a stranger from the distant past, the stakes are raised ever higher. "Dark and enthralling Christmas fable." *–NY Times.* "A timeless classic." *–Hollywood Reporter.* [5M] ISBN: 978-0-8222-2284-2

★ **THE NEW CENTURY by Paul Rudnick.** When the playwright is Paul Rudnick, expectations are geared for a play both hilarious and smart, and this provocative and outrageous comedy is no exception. "The one-liners fly like rockets." *–NY Times.* "The funniest playwright around." *–Journal News.* [2M, 3W] ISBN: 978-0-8222-2315-3

★ **SHIPWRECKED! AN ENTERTAINMENT—THE AMAZING ADVENTURES OF LOUIS DE ROUGEMONT (AS TOLD BY HIMSELF) by Donald Margulies.** The amazing story of bravery, survival and celebrity that left nineteenth-century England spellbound. Dare to be whisked away. "A deft, literate narrative." *–LA Times.* "Springs to life like a theatrical pop-up book." *–NY Times.* [2M, 1W] ISBN: 978-0-8222-2341-2

DRAMATISTS PLAY SERVICE, INC.
440 Park Avenue South, New York, NY 10016 212-683-8960 Fax 212-213-1539
postmaster@dramatists.com   www.dramatists.com